AUTHOR	İhsan Gümüş
CHIEF EDITOR	Oğuzhan Albayrak
FOREWORD	Prof. Christoph Bultmann
EDITING DIRECTOR	Dr. Arhan Kardas
EDITING TEAM	Dr. Frank Giesenberg,
	Brian D. Adams
DESIGN	Onur Alka

The rise of the
PALACE STATE
Turkey under the state of emergency

CONTENTS

ABBREVIATIONS X
EDITOR'S PREFACE XII
   About Oğuzhan Albayrak xv
FOREWORD XVI
INTRODUCTION XXXIV
   What is intended with this Book xxxiv
   Composition of the Book xxxvii
CHAPTER ONE 2
Living under the state of emergency 2
   Turkey's crackdown on its own citizens 3
   Regime and Society 7
CHAPTER TWO 12
Disturbing questions: from the "voiceless victims of the crises" in Turkey 12
   Country: Turkey 13
   Mercy vs. Mercilessness 15
   Families under the "Civic Death" conditions 16
   Dehumanization of children 18
   Sensitivity to the Suffering of "Others" 21
   Conclusion: Being the Voice of Voiceless 22
CHAPTER THREE 24
Decree laws as means of the revival of the "civil death" in Turkey . 24
   Hunger Strike 25
   "How Could There Be Such an Approach?" 26
   Civil Death Status Re-emerged 29
   No Need to "Behead These Traitors" 35
   Blacklisting Legalised: Cataloguing by State Agents .. 37
   Conclusion 40
CHAPTER FOUR 42
Erdoğan's asset forfeiture programme: weaponising decree laws in persecution of dissents 42
   Despotic Government 43
   Forfeiture in a Nutshell 44

Forfeiture in Turkey: A Brief History 45
Forfeiture in the Reign of Erdoğan 47
Decree Laws as a Means of Forfeiture 49
General Trustee: Savings Deposit Insurance Fund 54
Conclusion: Transition from the House of Prayers to the "Den of Robbers" 58

CHAPTER FIVE **60**
The commonwealth of Erdoğan: Milking public enterprises through Turkey wealth fund 60
Sovereign Wealth Funds 61
Turkey Wealth Fund (TWF) 65
Governance Framework 72
Operations and Investments 76
Auditing on Behalf of the Parliament 79
Conclusion: Theft is Property! 83

CHAPTER SIX **86**
The rise of "predatory government" in Turkey: An insight into the social background 86
Nature vs. Nurture 87
Predation in Human Gatherings 88
Predatory State 88
Political-sociological Dimension 90
Financial-economic Dimension 91
Erdoğanist Predation Methods 92
Toward a Predatory Regime in Turkey 95
Conclusion: Cultivating the Corruption in Society 106

CHAPTER SEVEN **108**
ECtHR: a new solution partner of the Erdoğan regime? 108
Burning Heretics with Low Cost 109
Controversies in the Judicial System 114
Judicial Innovation: A Non-Judicial Commission 116
At the Gate of the ECtHR 118
Erdoğan's Remedy Baptised by the ECtHR! 121
Criticism and CoE Response 123
Crossing the Red Sea 126

CHAPTER EIGHT **128**
Rule-with-violence: Emergence of the erdoğanist paramilitary in Turkey 128
    Erdoğan's Novelty: Setting the Repression *129*
    "Train-and-Equip" Program for the Jihadist Fighters: For What?.
    ....*132*
    SADAT: *Precursor to the Erdoğanist Death Squads* *142*
    Legislate-to-Kill: Immunity by the "Black Laws".............*153*
    Conclusions *159*

CHAPTER NINE **162**
The end of constitutional government 162
    Losers' Consent: "The Guy has won!".......................*163*
    Executive Presidency: "Chief Executive President" *166*
    State of Emergency Normalised *167*
    Legislature Underestimated. *172*
    The Executive Concentrated *176*
    Judiciary Packed *183*
    Ruling Party Subordinated *185*
    Rule of Law vs. Rule of Palace. *186*
    Returning to Ancient Times: Governing Without Government .*192*
    Electoral Autocracy: One Third of Democracy!. *194*
    Opposition: Losing Ground or Leading Change?. *197*
    Concluding Remarks *199*

REFERENCES **204**
INDEX... **212**
FIGURES **218**

LIST OF TABLES

Table 1: Forfeited Assets by Type and Numbers (2016–2017) 50
Table 2: Overall Financial Profile of the Companies Forfeited 55
Table 3: TWF-owned Companies with their Current Values 68
Table 4: Turkey in the Corruption Perception Indexes (2010–2017) ... 102
Table 5: Dismissals and Reinstates by Decree Laws (2016–2018) 112
Table 6: Dismissal of the Judges and Prosecutors by HSK (2016–2017) . 113
Table 7: Turkish Black Laws Enacted to Kill with Impunity 160
Table 8: The Laws Adopting Decree Laws Issued under the SoE 171
Table 9: Critical Institutions Affiliated / Linked to the Palatial Regime (2018) 183
Table 10: Changes in the Composition of the High Courts by Appointing Authorities 187

ABBREVIATIONS

AA	Anadolu Agency *(Anadolu Ajansı)*
AKP	Justice and Development Party *(Adalet ve Kalkınma Partisi)*
AYM	Turkish Constitutional Court *(Anayasa Mahkemesi)*
CHP	Republican People Party *(Cumhuriyet Halk Partisi)*
CoE	Council of Europe
EA	Electoral Authoritarianism
ECHR	European Convention on Human Rights
ECtHR	European Court of Human Rights
HDP	People's Democratic Party *(Halkların Demokratik Partisi)*
HSK	Council of Judges and Prosecutors *(Hakimler ve Savcılar Kurulu)*
(M)	The acronym "M" (*"Mükerrer"* in Turkish), in this book, refers to the "repeating" version(s) of the Official Gazette published with the same date and number.
MGK	National Security Council *(Milli Güvenlik Kurulu)*
MHP	Nationalist Action Party *(Milliyetçi Hareket Partisi)*
MİT	Turkish National Intelligence *(Milli İstihbarat Teşkilatı)*
MoD	Ministry of Defence

MP	Member of Parliament
OSCE	Organisation for Security and Cooperation in Europe
PM	Prime Ministry
PPJ	Platform for Peace and Justice
SADAT	International Defence Consultancy (SADAT Uluslararası Savunma Danışmanlık İnşaat Sanayi ve Ticaret A. Ş.)
SoE	State of Emergency
SSB	Chairmanship of Defence Industry (Savunma Sanayi Başkanlığı)
SWF	Sovereign Wealth Fund
TBMM	Grand National Assembly of Turkey (Türkiye Büyük Millet Meclisi)
TCPP	Turkish Code of Penal Procedure
TL	Turkish Lira
TMSF	Savings Deposit Insurance Fund (Tasarruf Mevduatı Sigorta Fonu)
TMV	Turkish Education Foundation (Türkiye Maarif Vakfı)
TRT	Radio & TV of Turkey (Türkiye Radyo ve Televizyon Kurumu)
TWF	Turkey Wealth Fund
YSK	Supreme Board of Election (Yüksek Seçim Kurulu)

EDITOR'S PREFACE

THIS BOOK IS ABOUT THE ECLIPSE OF HUMAN RIGHTS AND democracy in Turkey. As the Main Donau publishing house we thank in particular Oğuzhan Albayrak, a human rights activist, who revised and edited the text for the benefit of the English-speaking reader and updated the statistical data based on the current political and economic situation. As a doctor of human rights law, this book is very much also my personal concern. Our special thanks go to Professor Christoph Bultmann for his judicious foreword.

We as Main Donau publishing house feel a responsibility to act for the sake of human rights and freedoms, which is why we exceptionally publish the book in English in order to reach a broader public.

Arhan Kardas

15. August 2019

ABOUT OĞUZHAN ALBAYRAK

Having graduated from Public Administration, Oğuzhan Albayrak started his career as a diplomatic agent in the Ministry of Foreign Affairs of the Republic of Turkey in 2009. As a Junior Diplomat he served in the General-Directorate of Bilateral Political Affairs – Europe and General-Directorate for the European Union. He was assigned to posts in various embassies of Turkey in Kuwait, Malta, Jerusalem (Consulate General) and Azerbaijan, respectively. He was dismissed from his position in February 2017 as a result of the massive political purge by the Turkish government against dissidents. He is currently living in exile in Germany and is the Executive Director of the Human Rights Defenders e. V. (HRD) Association.

HRD is a non-profit and independent civil society organization campaigning to defend human rights and to help people facing persecution all around the world with a special focus on Turkey. HRD was established in 2018 in Cologne, Germany, by Turkish lawyers, former bureaucrats and entrepreneurs who are political asylum-seekers in Europe. HRD prepares reports concerning human rights violations, establishing contacts with other Human Rights NGOs and stakeholders, state officials and regional and international organizations. HRD also provides legal advice to victims, initiates legal procedures on behalf of the victims and prepares official petitions to the relevant UN Human Rights mechanisms.

FOREWORD

BY PROFESSOR CHRISTOPH BULTMANN

moral obtuseness is so much easier
(Martha Nussbaum, *Not for profit*, 2016)

THE PRESENT VOLUME BY İHSAN GÜMÜŞ, AN AUTHOR who, in a situation of persecution and oppression, writes under a pseudonym, is a collection of articles which were published on the website *Platform for Peace and Justice* in 2017 and 2018. They focus on the political development in Turkey following the military action, or attempted coup, on 15 July 2016 and the persecution of followers of Fethullah Gülen, i.e., the so-called Gülen movement. Gülen himself has been living in the US since March 1999, and readers may want to watch an interview, conducted by Tim Franks for the BBC Newshour on 27 January 2014, or read an interview, conducted by Jamie Tarabay and published in 'The Atlantic' on 14 August 2013, for a first impression of his teachings.[1] Excerpts from interviews over more than 20 years can be found in the

---

1. https://www.bbc.com/news/world-europe-25885817; https://www.theatlantic.com/international/archive/2013/08/a-rare-meeting-with-reclusive-turkish-spiritual-leader-fethullah-gulen/278662/.

book by Faruk Mercan, *No return from democracy. A survey of interviews with Fethullah Gülen* (2017).[2]

The articles by İhsan Gümüş are study material for scholars in the field of political sciences rather than for a theologian with an interest in interreligious dialogue. However, I have accepted the invitation to contribute a foreword to the present volume because it addresses an issue which I have also noticed myself: The almost complete silence in the media about the persecution of followers of Fethullah Gülen and the question of human rights in Turkey.

A few examples may illustrate this point, and since I cannot claim to have done a full survey of the debate in the media I prefer to put them as questions. In the German context: What can be read about the situation of followers of Gülen and the question of human rights in the weekly column 'Meine Türkei (My Turkey)' by Can Dündar in the newspaper 'Die Zeit'? In the French context: What can be read about the situation of followers of Gülen and the question of human rights in the occasional articles by Nedim Gürsel which have been collected in his book *Turquie libre, j'écris ton nom* (2018)? In the British context: What can be read about the situation of followers of Gülen and the question of human rights in the book by Ece Temelkuran, *How to lose a country. The 7 steps from democracy to dictatorship* (2019)?[3] With regard to publications like these, the collection of articles by İhsan Gümüş is a timely publication

---

2. German edition: *Kein Zurück von der Demokratie. M. Fethullah Gülen*, ed. by Faruk Mercan and Arhan Kardas, 2018, with an introduction by Arhan Kardas and a foreword which I contributed. The English edition contains an appendix with five articles by Gülen in the New York Times, Wall Street Journal, and Le Monde from February 2015 to August 2016. Meanwhile one more article in Le Monde of 26 February 2019 can be added to the list.
3. German edition: *Wenn dein Land nicht mehr dein Land ist. Oder sieben Schritte in die Diktatur*, 2019.

since it makes informations available which other authors do not share with their public.

To comment on day-to-day journalism from a scholar's point of view is always an awkward thing to do. The accusation of wanting to curb the freedom of the press or of demanding unreasonable standards of research or of pushing one particular and partisan opinion or of not understanding the risk of losing one's press card is easily at hand. From 2016 to 2018, I had the privilege of publishing a few contributions on the website *European Journalism Observatory* (EJO), so that readers of this foreword can find a number of critical observations on issues of journalism in relation to Turkey on this platform.[4] In addition, I would like to quote from the book by Anthony Lester, *Five ideas to fight for. How our freedom is under threat and why it matters* (2016), who writes:

> *Freedom of opinion and freedom of expression are the foundation for every free and democratic society. Free expression is a necessary condition to realise the principles of transparency and accountability we need to protect human rights. It is the basis for the full enjoyment of many other human rights, such as freedom of assembly and association and the right to vote. – No law and no court can save our right to free speech without the support of a strong, popular culture of liberty. (p. 142)*

In my understanding, Martha Nussbaum expresses the same concern with a 'strong, popular culture of liberty' when she states, in her preface to the 2016 edition of her book *Not for profit. Why democracy needs the humanities*:

---

4. https://de.ejo-online.eu/author/christoph-bultmann.

The humanities have been threatened since their very beginning. Socratic questioning is unsettling, and people in power often prefer docile followers to independent citizens able to think for themselves. Furthermore, a lively imagination, alert to the situations, desires, and sufferings of others is a taxing achievement; moral obtuseness is so much easier. So we should not be surprised that the humanities are under assault, now as ever. The battle for responsible democracy and alert citizenship is always difficult and uncertain. But it is both urgent and winnable, and the humanities are a large part of winning it. (p. xxiii)

In the light of statements such as these, there can be no question about the legitimate and necessary function of independent and critical journalism for strengthening 'responsible democracy'. At the same time, there should be limits to journalistic manipulations and campaigns; for this I like to refer to the *Code of Ethics* of the American *Society of Professional Journalists* (revised edition, 2014).[5]

The situation of followers of Gülen in Turkey and the question of human rights is not normally raised in debates about the political development of Turkey following the elections in 2011, because from 2014 the Turkish government has successfully pursued a propaganda campaign against the Gülen movement as a 'terrorist organization'. In 2015, some campaign advisor even invented the acronym 'FETÖ' (Fethullahçı Terör Örgütü) which at the time was duly commented on by the journalist Deniz Yücel in the German newspaper 'Die Welt' (15 September 2015). Nevertheless, this classification has not only filled the pages of Turkish newspapers ever since, but it has become so popular that the exiled journalist Can Dündar, in his column in the German newspaper 'Die Zeit' (no. 29/2019, of 13 June 2019),

---

5. https://www.spj.org/ethicscode.asp.

now even claims that the German chancellor has started to use it. The press conference, held on 28 September 2018 during a state visit of President Erdoğan in Berlin, to which he refers in order to support his assertion – and which is documented on the website of the German government[6] – shows that this journalistic claim is a gross manipulation.

In my view it remains a mystery why the diffamation of the Gülen movement has grown to such absurd proportions, since I take a pluralization within Islam through different reform movements as a natural development. In chapter 1, İhsan Gümüş convincingly states that 'Islamism acts as a destructive force against Islam itself'. Why should there only be one monolithic state Islam in Turkey, represented and directed by the Presidency of Religious Affairs (Diyanet)? Why should a 'political' Islam be a better religious option than a 'civil' Islam? Why should there not be room for a strand of Muslim piety based on teachings from the Sufi tradition? Why should believers not have a right to meet in the informal setting of a *sohbet*? Why should a secular worldview include the rejection of the human right of freedom of religion? And why should Muslims in diaspora communities not interact with Muslims in their home country or country of origin of their family as well as with Muslims in the society where they now live?

The Gülen movement, and more specifically the *Journalists and Writers Foundation* within the Gülen movement, founded in 1994, had started a series of conferences to address issues of Turkish society and politics in 1998 ('Abant conferences', normally concluding with an 'Abant declaration'). It is difficult to see, at least for someone who is not a political scientist, why this

---

6. https://www.bundesregierung.de/breg-de/suche/pressekonferenz-von-bundes kanzlerin-merkel-und-dem-tuerkischen-praesidenten-recep-tayyip-erdo%C4%-9Fan-1532384.

line of engagement has not been more productive for all those who participated in it. For someone who tries, with an interdisciplinary interest, to understand the situation in Turkey, there are many interesting books to consult such as Ahmet Insel, *La nouvelle Turquie d'Erdogan. Du rêve démocratique à la derive autoritaire* (2015, 2nd edn. 2017), or Ece Temelkuran, *Turkey. The insane and the melancholy* (2015),[7] or Sevim Dagdelen, *Der Fall Erdogan. Wie uns Merkel an einen Autokraten verkauft* (2016), or Inga Rogg, *Türkei, die unfertige Nation. Erdoğans Traum vom Osmanischen Reich* (2017), or Hasnain Kazim, *Krisenstaat Türkei. Erdoğan und das Ende der Demokratie am Bosporus* (2017). Yet the question why the persecution of followers of Fethullah Gülen is abandoned to almost complete silence in the media remains a disconcerting question.

One reason for this silence is, of course, the military action, or attempted coup, on 15 July 2016, which, in the public debate, is still a puzzle, since the preferences for ascribing the responsibility for this military action or attempted coup to whomever are never supported by sufficient evidence. In his book *How democracy ends* (2018), David Runciman, political scientist in Cambridge, writes in a chapter "Coup!" (in which Turkey only figures as a marginal issue):

> *The attempted coup of July 2016 can simultaneously be held up as evidence of two diametrically opposed threats to democracy. If it is taken at face value, the threat comes from the military: Turkish democracy is still weak enough that it could be overthrown by force. But if the coup is assumed to be fake, then the threat comes from the democratically elected government: Turkish democracy is now secure enough that popular support becomes the cover for would-be autocrats*

---

7. German edition: *Euphorie und Wehmut. Die Türkei auf der Suche nach sich selbst*, 2015.

to hide behind. There is nothing – no event, no argument, no piece of evidence – that can determine to the satisfaction of all parties which view is correct. (p. 53)

However, even if so-called 'dark forces' within the Gülen movement in Turkey should have been involved in the planning of a coup – at whatever level of initiative or cooperation or persuasion or deception –, it is clear that the number of coup plotters does not amount to hundreds and thousands. Yet the victims of persecution and oppression are counted in tens and hundreds of thousands, families included. In his articles, İhsan Gümüş provides – at least to a high degree – a realistic picture of the situation of these victims and the 'predatory practices' which makes life in Turkish society almost impossible for them. On a more personal note I would like to quote a statement from a correspondence in June 2016 with a competent, yet anything but neutral critic of the Gülen movement who stated at the time:

I have no doubt that the vast majority of Gulen's sympathizers are well-intentioned and would want to have no part in the kind of machinations I am talking about. I would not want to accuse millions for the sins of what appears to be a small group within the movement. It should be clear that my accusations are directed against this group rather than everyone associated with the movement.

The suggested differentiation seems to have very little impact on debates when the question of human rights is concerned. Given the competition for education, status, income, and influence in Turkish society between the numerous milieus – some more established, some more marginal – in this society, I wonder how far the issue of political emotions plays a role here. An enlightening discussion of such emotions is offered, for example, by Martha Nussbaum in her book *Political emotions. Why love matters for justice* (2013), especially the chapter 'Compassion's enemies: Fear, envy, shame'. Nussbaum writes:

> *[...] we need to ask what more can be done to support a culture of civic friendship that makes people less likely, at least, to be at odds with one another in this way. Envy attacks compassion in two ways: by narrowing the circle of concern and thus encouraging the 'eudaimonistic thought' to focus on the self, or one's own group, and by inhibiting the sense of similar possibilities and the empathy that usefully accompanies it, suggesting that the envied are 'other' or 'the enemy.' (p. 345)*

In a professional scholarly study of the communication, in the media as well as in scholarship, about the Gülen movement and the question of human rights it would be an interesting point to consider how a differentiation between 'the vast majority of Gulen's sympathizers' and 'a small group within the movement' does or does not inform the reporting about and discussion of the situation in Turkey and what evidence is presented for allegations relating to this internal so-called 'small group'.[8]

The author İhsan Gümüş also addresses the issue of the international reaction to the political development in Turkey since July 2016. Thus, in chapter 1, he refers to the European Union and the Council of Europe. It would again be a challenge for political scientists to analyse the relevant documents which have been offered to the public so far. Within the framework of the Council of Europe – which is founded on the *European*

---

8. See also the postscript 'The predicament of the Gülen movement in the aftermath of the July 15th coup attempt' in Anwar Alam, *For the sake of Allah. The origin, development, and discourse of the Gülen movement*, 2019, 271-94.

Convention of Human Rights –, the Commissioner for Human Rights has commented on the situation in Turkey in his/her four 'Quarterly Activity Reports' per year as well as his/her 'Annual Activity Report'; these reports can be found on the respective website.[9] The Parliamentary Assembly of the Council of Europe (PACE) passed a resolution on Turkey on 25 April 2017 (Resolution 2156: 'The functioning of democratic institutions in Turkey') which again can be found on the respective website.[10] The resolution (which cannot be quoted in full here)[11] contains statements such as:

[Article 7] Unfortunately, eight months after the attempted coup, the situation has deteriorated and measures have gone far beyond what is necessary and proportionate. The authorities have been ruling through decree laws going far beyond what emergency situations require and overstepping the parliament's legislative competence. The Assembly is also concerned that most of the decree laws have so far not been approved (as required by the constitution), or their implementation monitored by the parliament, which it considers to be a serious democratic deficiency.

[Article 14] The Assembly expresses its deep concern about the scale and extent of the purges conducted in the public administration and the judiciary, and many other public institutions, targeting alleged members of the Gülen movement. The Assembly recalls its Resolution 2121 (2016) and notes that the Gülen movement, a former ally of the ruling party operating legally until 2014, was later labelled

---

9. https://www.coe.int/en/web/commissioner/activity-reports.
10. http://assembly.coe.int/nw/xml/XRef/Xref-DocDetails-EN.asp?fileid=23665&lang=EN.
11. Resolution 2156 consists of 40 sections and contains important sections on the persecution and oppression of the Kurdish population and representatives of the parliamentary party HDP in Turkey.

as the "Fethullahist Terrorist Organisation"/"Parallel State Structure" and considered a terrorist organisation. According to the Venice Commission, while civil servants have an obligation to be loyal to the State and not to take instructions from external sources, it is the duty of the State to clarify to all public servants when a hitherto well-established organisation is subsequently considered a "threat to the national security" – and becomes thus incompatible with public service – to avoid lack of information and clarity which could lead to "unjust dismissals which may be seen as retroactive punishment".

[Article 16] The Assembly is extremely worried about the high number of individuals arrested and kept in custody waiting indictment, without access to their files. The Assembly expects the Turkish authorities to resort to pretrial detention only as a last resort and on valid grounds.

[Article 17] The Assembly is also dismayed by the social consequences of the measures applied in the framework of the state of emergency. The civil servants who were dismissed have had their passports cancelled. They are banned from ever working again in the public administration, or in institutions which have links to the administration. They have no access to a social security scheme and their assets have been seized – which raises the question of the protection of property rights. Their families have also been affected by these measures. The Assembly fears that these measures amount to a "civil death", for those concerned. This situation will have a dramatic and detrimental long-term effect on Turkish society, which will need to find the means and mechanisms to overcome this trauma.

[Article 20] The Assembly remains worried about respect for fundamental rights under the state of emergency. Considering the scale of the operations undertaken, the Assembly is concerned that the *state of emergency has been used not only to remove those involved in the coup from the State institutions, but also to silence any critical voices and create a climate of fear among ordinary citizens, academics, independent non-governmental organisations (NGOs) and the media, jeopardising the foundations of a democratic society.*

[Article 25] With respect to freedom of the media and of expression, the Assembly is alarmed by the repeated violations of the former, the large number of journalists currently detained and the pressure exerted on critical journalists: these are unacceptable in a democratic society. Council of Europe member States have a positive obligation to ensure freedom of expression, the protection of journalists and access to information, and to create conditions enabling the media to act as public or social watchdogs and inform the public on matters of general and public interest.

[Article 27] The Assembly thus calls on the Turkish authorities to

27.1. release all detained journalists (more than 150) and human rights defenders;

27.2. put an end to the unacceptable policy of the criminalisation of dissenting voices, and protect media freedom, in line with the European Convention on Human Rights and the case law of the European Court of Human Rights; review the attitudes and practices of members of the justice system, in particular prosecutors and peace judges, so as to discard the "consistent pattern of judicial harassment with a clear chilling effect that stifles criticism" (as described by the Commissioner for Human Rights) and to achieve a more Convention-compliant interpretation of Turkish legislation;

27.3. amend the anti-terror law so as to ensure that its implementation and interpretation comply with the European Convention on Human Rights;

27.4. refrain from applying sweeping measures, including against the media, academics and NGOs, on the basis of vague criteria of alleged "connection" to a terrorist organisation without evidentiary grounds and in the absence of judicial decisions;

27.5. ensure that the Inquiry Commission on State of Emergency Measures will be fully operational without further delay and with the power to restore the status quo ante and/or, where appropriate, provide adequate compensation; grant priority treatment to the most urgent applications, including those introduced by the media outlets; and issue reasoned, individualised decisions in line with the recent opinions of the Venice Commission;

27.6. create an environment conducive to media freedom and pluralism, notably by strengthening the editorial independence of the Turkish Radio and Television Broadcasting Company, and implementing an effective monitoring mechanism to ensure that the media abides with regulations, in line with Council of Europe standards.

The resolution was, however, adopted *against* the votes of the delegates from Turkey who represented the three parties AKP, MHP, and CHP; only the delegates of the HDP supported the resolution.[12] It would again be a matter for political scientists to explain the consensus between the three parties AKP, MHP, and CHP in their alternative understanding of the human rights situation in Turkey. For further developments within the Council

---

12. For the votes see: http://assembly.coe.int/nw/xml/Votes/DB-VotesResults-EN.asp?VoteID=36533&DocID=16218&MemberID=.

of Europe readers must be referred directly to documents on the website of this institution.[13]

As far as the European Union is concerned, the main documents to mention are resolutions of the European Parliament.[14] Only three of these can be highlighted in the present context: The resolution of 6 July 2017 'on the 2016 Commission Report on Turkey', the resolution of 8 February 2018 'on the current human rights situation in Turkey', and the resolution of 13 March 2019 'on the 2018 Commission Report on Turkey'.[15] At least in the German context, most of these resolutions have never been brought to the attention of the public which shows a blatant disregard on the side of journalism for the work of members of the European Parliament. Again on a more personal note, I would like to mention an editorial comment in the 'Süddeutsche Zeitung' of 2 April 2019 which carried the headline 'Turkey. Democracy is alive' ('Türkei. Die Demokratie lebt'). Whoever studies the resolutions of the European Parliament will find it difficult to agree with the journalist and the editor who accepted the piece for the opinion page.

---

13. See the press release of 5 April 2018 about a fact-finding visit to Turkey from 28 to 30 March 2018 by the co-rapporteurs for the monitoring of Turkey by the Parliamentary Assembly of the Council of Europe (PACE), Marianne Mikko (Estonia, SOC) and Nigel Evans (United Kingdom, EC) (http://assembly.coe.int/nw/xml/News/News-View-en.asp?newsid=7013&lang=2) and their report of 17 June 2018 (http://website-pace.net/documents/19887/4268449/AS-MON-2018-07-EN.pdf/3b75884c-6a63-46cb-b366-f902732df2b2) which was released on 26 June 2018 (http://assembly.coe.int/nw/xml/News/News-View-en.asp?newsid=7140&lang=2). – See also the press release about a visit to Turkey by the Commissioner for Human Rights of 8 July 2019 (https://www.coe.int/en/web/commissioner/-/turkey-needs-to-put-an-end-to-arbitrariness-in-the-judiciary-and-to-protect-human-rights-defenders).
14. See http://www.europarl.europa.eu/delegations/en/d-tr/documents/ep-resolutions.
15. See http://www.europarl.europa.eu/doceo/document/TA-8-2017-0306_EN.html?redirect, http://www.europarl.europa.eu/doceo/document/TA-8-2018-0040_EN.html?redirect, http://www.europarl.europa.eu/doceo/document/TA-8-2019-0200_EN.pdf?redirect.

The concern with informations about the situation in Turkey which informs the articles by İhsan Gümüş can also be followed in materials published, for example, by *Amnesty International*[16] or *Human Rights Watch*. A few paragraphs from the 'World Report 2019' of Human Rights Watch will show what picture of the situation can be gained from these documents. The authors write in their country report on Turkey:[17]

Terrorism charges continued to be widely used. As of June [2018], almost one-fifth (48,924) of the total prison population (246,426) had been charged with or convicted of terrorism offences, according to the Ministry of Justice. Those prosecuted and convicted included journalists, civil servants, teachers, and politicians, as well as police officers and military personnel.

Of the 48,924, 34,241 were held for alleged Gulenist (FETÖ) links, and 10,286 for alleged links to the outlawed Kurdistan Workers' Party (PKK), and 1,270 for alleged links to the extremist Islamic State (ISIS) group.

Many terrorism trials in Turkey lack compelling evidence of criminal activity or acts that would reasonably be deemed terrorism, and the practice of holding individuals charged with terrorism offenses in prolonged pretrial detention raised concerns its use has become a form of summary punishment.

The present book confronts the reader with a difficult question: What can be done to support the victims of persecution and oppression in Turkey? What can be done to break the

---

16. See especially 'Turkey: Weathering the storm: Defending human rights in Turkey's climate of fear' of 26 April 2018 (https://www.amnesty.org/en/documents/eur44/8200/2018/en/).
17. See https://www.hrw.org/world-report/2019/country-chapters/turkey.

admiration for the Turkish government's 'FETÖ' campaign? What can be done to give the tens of thousands who have fallen victim to the Turkish government a new life? What can be done to inspire more voices in Turkey and abroad with an orientation towards human rights as they are expressed, for example, in the *European Convention on Human Rights*? What can be done in the interest of peacebuilding and peace education in Turkey and beyond? What can be done to have a fruitful debate about the foundation upon which religions can flourish in a peaceful, pluralistic, modern world of human rights, freedom of religion, and responsible democracy? The book by İhsan Gümüş provides informations about the chain of actions which has led to the continuing situation of crisis. This is an important first step.

The book comes at a favourable moment. In the German context, a better understanding of the reality of persecution in Turkey has been made possible through the book by Ahmet Altan, *Ich werde die Welt nie wiedersehen. Texte aus dem Gefängnis* (2018). The book is also available in an English version, *I will never see the world again* (2019), with a compelling foreword by Philippe Sands. Another author and great writer to think of is Aslı Erdoğan, whose *Nicht einmal das Schweigen gehört uns noch* (2017)[18] and *Das Haus aus Stein* are amazing documents of humanity and wisdom. The preface to the German translation of *Das Haus aus Stein* of January 2019 evokes the author's own experience as a prisoner in Turkey. The journalist Meşale Tolu has published a report on her time in prison, as a young mother together with her child, from April to December 2017: *"Mein Sohn bleibt bei mir!". Als politische Geisel in türkischer Haft – und warum es noch nicht zu Ende ist* (2019). The forthcoming book by Deniz Yücel, *Agentterrorist*.

---

18. French edition: *Le silence même n'est plus à toi*, 2017; the German edition has a foreword by Cem Özdemir.

Eine Geschichte über Freiheit und Freundschaft, Demokratie und Nichtsodemokratie (2019) will be a significant addition to this list.[19]

A democracy is a country in which power is held by elected representatives – this is one of the most basic definitions of a democratic state. The political system of a democracy can only work if freedom of the media, tied to high standards of media ethics, and free and fair elections are guaranteed. The political system of a democracy can only work if the elected representatives know what their responsibilities are. No democracy, no constitutional system that is orientated towards the protection of human rights can work 'without the support of a strong, popular culture of liberty'. The book by İhsan Gümüş has the potential to motivate people who want to live in freedom and want to see others live in freedom to overcome moral obtuseness.

---

19. Meanwhile see his *Wir sind ja nicht zum Spaß hier. Reportagen, Satiren und andere Gebrauchstexte*, ed. by Doris Akrap, 2017.

INTRODUCTION

WHAT IS INTENDED WITH THIS BOOK

This book is born of articles (they were seven in sum) that appeared on the Platform for Peace and Justice (PPJ) in 2017 – 18. Following their original publication, these articles, with a scrutiny of relevance and an update of the matters according to the course of events, have now been turned into the chapters of this very book. Therefore, each chapter says more than what the former articles said.

Online governmental and media archives were also critical for this book. I therefore gave the relevant links to the press news and legislative sources like Official Gazette, public announcements, media reports etc. I may be wrong, but it is my worry that the regime, in the near future, might prevent researchers from having access to such links and sources.

For the sake of readability, I have tried to avoid cluttering the text with footnotes or excessive references, quotations, and citation marks. Instead, I provided the reader with a detailed list of the decree laws issued during the State of Emergeny (SoE) (Table 8). Yet details (publication date and publication number in the Official Gazette) of other laws which I am referring to in the book can be traced from the footnotes. Through various tables, I tried to summarise the size of forfeiture and predation operations in monetary terms. I hope this approach, more or less, will allow further studies of researchers as well as providing an easy reference. I also believe it is a necessary moral endeavour.

In doing so, namely, working with a huge amount of legal documents, referring to dates and numbers through tables and footnotes, what concerned me was the following: although it all happened before our eyes, the events and conditions might be forgotten in a world on the move. Then, researchers, for example when studying the SoE regime, may find it difficult to consider the relevance of the documents and to connect the legislative operations with the actual cases. This may also be the case in the assessment of the original intentions at that time.

The prevailing aim of this book is not to show the atrocities which many Turkish citizens experienced during the SoE, but rather to deepen our knowledge and understanding of authoritarianism, to provide an up-to-date explanation of its roots, and to offer our thoughts on how a better foundation for an electoral democracy could be constructed in the future.

To this end, I rather examined consequences of the organised legislative operations (i. e. deliberate complication of domestic remedies, revival of civil death, black laws, immunity- impunity, forfeiture and predation strategies, paramilitary formations, normalcy of the SoE, court packing, concentration of power etc.) that have received less attention of scholars, lawyers and journalists most of whom focused on the justification of the operations in question.

My analyses have involved, to a large extent, a great deal of documentary research on the legal evidences against ill-fabricated narratives of the regime such as infiltration into the state, encroaching upon the army, orchestrating the coup attempt of 15 July 2016 etc. That is why the book provides great numbers of references, footnotes, and lists of legislations indicating that the servants of the regime worked hard to legitimize organised crimes like theft, plundering, murder, violence, and persecution. Within this book, I will demonstrate that "grand corruptions" (see chapter 6) and politically organised crimes have been documented even by the perpetrators themselves in the form of black laws, decrees, circulars, judicial decisions and so forth.

Thus, the question of "what was the crime" finally appears to have met its answer: The crime is to steal, to forfeit in a predatory manner, to kill with impunity on behalf of the state, nation, faith, religion. It is also the crime to dismiss people without any judicial proceedings and to jail pregnant women, mothers and their children without any medical and/or obstetric care. But what is not a crime is for people to choose a bank to deposit their money with, to choose a school for their children to attend, to choose smartphone apps to communicate, to subscribe to a daily newspaper etc. Finally, it is not a crime to be a voice of dissent to an incumbent president.

Anyway, it is my hope that this book will reveal a certain set of Palatial persecution and predation practices and their effects that proliferate every day. Of course, I am not naive enough to expect that it will change the course of events. But if it moves even one person to act or speak out against this corrupted regime, or think about their responsibilities as a human being or scholar, it will be an asset for the future.

As a last word, the reader should bear in mind that the author writes from a country where some mothers can only access prenatal or postnatal care behind bars; a country where common sense has been silenced by brutality, and where persecution by the regime has increased to an overwhelming degree; a country with the lowest Freedom House score (2018) that brings it to the "Not Free" status.

COMPOSITION OF THE BOOK

The form of this book is not so much a strictly rational or pedagogical order, but a lecture on something less known in the academic realm. It begins with a murder: the murder of basic human rights in Turkey, with the most disappointing connivance of the ECtHR, and ends with a controversial election victory of Erdoğan on 24 June 2018. Therefore, despite some occasional jokes here and there, the chapters have not been very enjoyable to write, and I am afraid the book will also not be enjoyable to read.

Chapter 1 attempts to give an insight into the nature of the regime's crackdown on its own citizens as well as providing some methodological points guiding the author throughout the study. In doing this, I do not intend to tell a story that received little media attention in Turkey, but to demonstrate how the "three *dispositifs* of law, discipline, and security," in Foucaultian sense,[1] have been distorted through "Organised Legislative Operations." Indeed, all the chapters, to some extent, show how the regime has gradually replaced these principles with their opposites: unlawfulness, no discipline, and insecurity, respectively.

Chapter 2 is concerned with the traumas that pregnant women, mothers and children experienced under the SoE. We asked some questions – not hoping – to be replied by the regime in Turkey on the conditions of these people whose lives were

---

1. M. Foucault (1926 – 1984) explains the term *dispositif* as "a system of relations between elements," which includes "discourses, institutions, architectural forms, regulatory decisions, laws, administrative measures, scientific statements, philosophical, moral, and philanthropic propositions" and their operations and interconnections in a realm (Dean, 2013).

torn apart by the violence and can never again be made whole. Apart from the stance of the regime, less sympathy shown by society to the stories of these people was also noted. So, in a country with an overwhelming Muslim majority that has been voted a "pious" man, Erdoğan, for years, we talk about pregnant women and babies held in jail despite exact disapproval of both national and universal provisions. Indeed, there are no words to describe it.

Contrary to its title, not the questions but the stories are much disturbing in this chapter. Yet, making the effects of the crackdown long lasting for all those who may pose a threat to the regime could be best achieved in practice through revival of the "civil death."

Chapter 3 explores the implications of disenfranchisements subsequent to mass dismissals. In doing so, I attempt to demonstrate – more or less – the similarities between the "civil death", a *Medieval* notion of judicial realm and conditions under which the victims of SoE in Turkey have been enforced to live (or die!).

I itemized the disenfranchisements within the decree laws and showed how the sum total of these restrictions may turn ordinary citizens, as V. Das and D. Poole (2004) offered, to "killable bodies" without punishment if they are blacklisted as the ones who are not worthy to "exist" in civil realm: Eleven (11) major restrictions in total ranging from cancellation of passports to refusal of burial services making the stigmatised bodies vulnerable to assault, torture, rape, and killing! Their entirety appears to be equal to civil death.

Chapter 4 portrays the operations of the regime aiming at the complete economic devastation of dissenting groups. In addition to the "trustee" appointment procedure allowed by the Turkish Code of Penal Procedure (TCPP) right after the coup attempt, the regime introduced a series of decree laws to ensure direct forfeiture of the assets allegedly belonging to Gülen linked organisations like schools, hospitals, universities, and so forth. Further to this, blacklisted companies and individual enterprises were also transferred into the portfolio of the Savings Deposit Insurance Fund" (TMSF) designated as a kind of General Trustee. Official reports say that, by 2018, assets belonging to 4.911 organisations are held by the National Estates while trustees – fully or partly – are in control of 1.207 companies with an asset value of 52.8 billion TL (appr. $10 billion at that time) some of which are sectoral leaders. The latter has been put gradually under liquidation for sale to pro-AKP "entrepreneurs".

Chapter 5 aims to analyse what I have labelled as "milking public enterprises" through TWF. TWF was established by Law no. 6741 in August 2016 with the apparent aim of "contributing to the diversity and depth of the capital market instruments, bringing the public assets of the country into the economy," and so on. However, when we review the literature looking contemporary models, we learn that "Sovereign Wealth Funds" (SWFs), in principle, are established to ensure better utilisation of "economic surpluses" of countries.

However, without relying on any surplus such as revenues extracted from a particular natural source, i. e. oil and gas, and excess foreign exchange reserves and budget contributions, TWF was devised as an administrative apparatus to squeeze out every bit of productive capacity from the national resources and to funnel them into unproductive realms in a non-transparent manner. As of today (December 2018), 14 public enterprises with about $6.3 billion of equity capital and appr. $200 billion of asset size by 2017, plus large number of real estate (appr. 2.3 million square meter) and licenses generating high revenues with almost no cost are under the control of the TWF headed personally by Erdoğan and his son-in-law.

This chapter also shows that organisational structure and operations assigned to TWF by its internal regulation largely contradicts with the rules of game codified within the Santiago Principles of October 2008. As such, TWF is a product of decay of Turkish political economy and governance frameworks and provides adequate evidence of Erdoğan's continued commitment to predation of the public assets. Yet TWF means little for a "predatory" ruler as we shall examine in greater depth in the next chapter.

Chapter 6 looks into the background of the predatory strategies and contemporary forms of predatory leadership as well as various methods of predation developed by the regime in the last decade. We suggest the key word in any analysis of the Erdoğan regime is "predatory" because the term "corruption" (Transparency International, however, offers the term "Grand Corruption") has already remained deficient to describe the affairs with their entirety since the failed coup of 15 July.

Our analyses point to the conclusion that, relying on the legally-organised practices like predation and forfeiture as the "clean" forms of robbery; systematic milking the economy for private gains has become the norm for Erdoğan and his political supporters. Over his political career, Erdoğan extended his personal ownership to practically almost every economic sector in Turkey including heavy-cost infrastructure projects. He owned controlling interests in mining, mass housing, shipping, media outlets, construction companies, hotels, and government-owned banks.

In sum, I identified three main pillars as the ones over which the Erdoğanist predatory state rises: (1) misuse of the spiritual power of Islam in hearts and minds, (2) political economy that couples high growth rates with persistent poverty, but prevents poor from becoming independent in the sense of financial well-being at the same time, and finally (3) highly polarised conditions of Turkish society as a key to maintaining predatory goals over the country and to keeping social-political groupings away from evolving to become "social movements" (see below). The latter generally promotes collective violence because, as Tilly (2003) suggests, it makes the "us-them" boundary more salient, hollows out the uncommitted middle, intensifies conflicts across the boundary, raises the stakes of winning or losing, and enhances opportunities for leaders to initiate action against their enemies. That is what the chapter 8 is about: paramilitary power.

Chapter 7 starts with the review of sample ECtHR decisions concerning the predicaments from which the victims of SoE in Turkey still try to exit: reinstate to jobs, proper financial redress, removal of restrictions, recovery of property, etc. I argue that decisions in question were purposely devised to abandon the suffering people to their fates and to leave no exit in judicial sense. Opinion No. 865/2016 of the Venice Commission (2016) is an evidence of the collusive agreement between Ankara and Strasbourg.

Thus, the punishment I mentioned above has gained a kind of lifelong character. In this vein, the regime in Ankara complicated the judicial remedy system through decree laws while the ECtHR, recognizing the regime's administrative hoax (a "Commission" with no redressing capacity) as a "remedy" that needs to be exhausted before the courts, opened an escape corridor for itself from review of thousands of application files. When it comes to the basic question of "what is the crime," the ECtHR appeared to adopt a tactic of "touch-and-go." Turkey's crackdown on its own citizens has thus turned into a reputational risk of the ECtHR in Strasbourg.

The interactions between the Council of Europe (CoE), the ECtHR, Venice Commission and the regime taught us how judicial review of Human Rights violations could be postponed for an uncertain time when political preferences of the regime met with the "practical" concerns ("to keep the dam to be broken," see chapter 2) of the CoE and the ECtHR's judges at the cost of deepening the desperation of victims in Turkey.

That was one of the major achievements of the regime to intimidate the victims and potential opposition to the regime's survival. But the worst is yet to come: jailing mothers and pregnant women as a proven way of intimidation throughout history.

Chapter 8 attempts to discover the underlying conditions of the emergence of the pro-Erdoğan paramilitary in the form of death squads and vigilant groups as a repressive machine against dissent.

As could be observed, taking the occasion of SoE, the regime, through Islamist and nationalist narratives, has turned the violence into a social and cultural resource that can be practical and instrumental or symbolic and expressive. This was to ensure that persecutions of the regime could evoke so little opposition, so much consent across the society and less sympathy for the victims.

Also taking the opportunity of the instability in Syria, he has invested a huge amount of money in the organisation of the *jihadist* fighter groups under the so-called "Train-and-Equip" program while translating "provisional village guards" of the South-eastern into permanent "security guards."

It seems to me that limited killing capacity of the regular army forces due to legal framework, ultimately may led the regime to invoke some patriotic formations like mercenary terrorists, vigilant groups, or death squads without the constraints of being a government entity. Seen from this angle, SADAT-type organisations cannot simply be considered as private entities competing in the market, but rather the ones designed to serve as the structural and conceptual precursor for Erdoğan's paramilitary groups linked with the State by their decisiveness to stop whatever potential success the opposition might have.

Chapter 9 is devoted to the analysis of another hot objective of interest in public and social science at the turn of the country within the context of the 24 June elections putting also the constitutional amendments of April 2017 into force: "Executive Presidency" that I called as the "Palatial Regime" or Palace-State. Given the arbitrary concentration of the powers at the Palace and distortion of the "public" characters of the governmental structures, it is safe to conclude that this regime represents an *archaic* and outmoded imaginary of an omnipotent sovereignty that is incompatible with democratic governance.

This chapter sets forth a concept of Palatial regime that involves a neatly organised structure of dependency and control as a kind of *antithesis* to the contemporary forms of the state and is, as such, comparable only to its ancient samples in the Middle East. I suggest that the rise of the palace as a power centre in a country is closely associated with the rise of authoritarianism.

I therefore call this political system not a governmental, but an electoral regime with *autocratic* features in which a ruler governs without government. It is "the death of the constitutional government" in a usual sense because it gives way to wholesale subordination to the will of the ruler who answers neither to the parliament nor to the public.

CHAPTER ONE
Living under the state of emergency

> *They make a desert and call it peace.*
> Tacitus (56 – 120 BC)

TURKEY'S CRACKDOWN ON ITS OWN CITIZENS

MY EXPERIENCE WAS NOT UNUSUAL INDEED. IN many ways, mine was just one of the stories of hundred thousands of Turkish people who were caught up in the awful monster of mass dismissal, dispossession, arbitrary detention, interrogation, and even torture that followed an alleged coup attempt on the evening of July 15, 2016.

At the top level of the security and intelligence bureaucracy, it had been an open secret, shared by all, that the regime, being supported by a large contingent of an Ultranationalist and Islamist alliance, had for a long time been planning to teach the Gülen Movement a brutal lesson about the true nature of the state which the movement had allegedly infiltrated.

On the very evening, when the dust had not yet settled, Erdoğan and his allies accused the *Gülen Movement* of being the real force behind the coup attempt. It was the Gülen sympathizers that the regime took to be the culprits – even though their involvement in the coup attempt has even now not been established by any substantial evidence.[1]

In the immediate aftermath of the abortive coup, the regime, with the Cabinet Decree no.2016/9064,[2] declared a country-wide "State of Emergency" (SoE) on 21 July 2016 and organized a campaign intended to destroy the movement and its affiliates. Through a carefully crafted media campaign, Erdoğan dehumanized and demonized sympathizers of the Gülen Movement and called for them to be eliminated "down to the roots." Thus, he gave license to the judges, prosecutors, police chiefs, and all enemies of the Gülenists to break the rule of law in this vein.

Right after the introduction of the SoE, thousands of civil servants including soldiers, judges and prosecutors started to be sacked by decree laws or executive orders to which blacklists were appended. Dismissals were followed by mass detention and jailing of these civil servants under the allegation of links to the Gülen Movement as well as the permanent closure of private institutions, such as foundations, schools, hospitals, universities, trade and labor unions, media outlets, and so forth, and this closure resulted in the confiscation of all the properties owned by these institutions.

Arrest operations extended to lawyers representing detainees and journalists criticizing the happenings. Meanwhile many high-ranking soldiers appeared in the media with their tortured or harshly beaten images. But the worst was yet to come: security forces started to detain women just before or immediately after giving birth. The worst of all possibilities was coming true. Widespread violence and overcrowding in prisons became one

---

1. For some factual information about the controversial coup attempt, see the following: http://stockholmcf.org/a-new-report-in-sweden-reveals-erdogan-orchestrated-july-15-coup-in-turkey/(Accessed: 10 July 2017).
2. Cabinet Decree no. 2016/9064 was published in the Official Gazette of 21 July 2016, with no. 29 777.

of the most prominent markers of the SoE while some victims ultimately turned into asylum seekers fleeing economic hardship and insecurity.

The scope of the purge rapidly went beyond the Gülen Movement, and government action targeted citizens who were suspected of having ties to the "usual suspects" in Turkey such as the Revolutionary People's Liberation Party-Front (DHKP-C), the Kurdistan Workers Party (PKK), and its affiliated organisation, the Kurdistan Communities Union (KCK).

The Minister of Interior and provincial governors in the south-eastern part of the country, relying on the Decree Law no. 674 of 1 September 2016, started to appoint "trustees" (*kayyım* in Turkish) *in lieu* of elected mayors, deputy mayors or members of municipal assemblies. Not surprisingly, all those who were replaced were of Kurdish origin and dismissed or arrested with the accusation of terrorism. By the end of 2017, 94 trustees occupied the municipal offices while 68 former mayors were imprisoned.[3]

Also, relying on the legal shield granted by the Law no. 6722 of 14 July 2016 (attention should be paid to the date of introduction!), special operation teams launched a semi-genocidal campaign and atrocities in the South-East region of the country. The bombardments were followed by a mass expulsion and the destruction of homes to discourage displaced people from returning.

All this was arranged to avoid the impression of a civil war. Rather it was one of the largest and swiftest instances of mass dismissal, arrest, incarceration and state terror on a scale never seen before in the history of the country. Yet no one from the

---

3. See, for example: https: //tr. euronews. com/2017/12/11/kayyum-raporu-102-belediyenin-94une-kayyum-atandi (Accessed: 27 11. 2018).

"Gülen community" took up arms, regardless of the extraordinary nature of the crackdown which they collectively faced.

Meanwhile many international organisations like the European Union (EU) and the Council of Europe (CoE), as well as influential government leaders, on several occasions – for example in their reports or press releases – criticised the impact of Turkey's crackdown on dissent of all kinds, albeit in a diplomatic language. Despite numerous pieces of evidence that would suffice to pave the way for Erdoğan to be put in the dock at The Hague they remained bystanders. Erdoğan in his turn replied to them by saying that "the courts are independent in their decisions."

Although pro-Erdoğan prosecutors and law enforcement bodies joined the campaign in the sense of formal procedures, it was also aided and abetted by radical Islamist groups, *tariqats*, media outlets, Ultranationalist ideologues and the secular part of left-wing constituencies, and politicians on both sides of the aisle were absorbed into it with little vacillation between two poles. *(See figure 1, page 220)*

As a result, the two-years SoE rule that formally ended on 18 July 2018 left behind numerous migrants escaping death, more than a hundred thousand of job seekers prohibited from public employment, imprisonment of people for indeterminate periods, mothers and babies in jail, widespread violence and overcrowding in prisons, and so forth. It left behind over a hundred thousand people and their families living in conditions of civil death, deprived of their jobs, vocational qualifications, licenses, passports etc.

The events under the SoE regime negatively affected the lives of many thousands of people who were officially stigmatized only because of their familial or other association with those who were arbitrarily dismissed or detained. Worse still, the

Palatial regime appears to continue prosecuting, arresting, and jailing enough Gülen affiliated persons so that the survivors of these campaigns can no longer pose a conceivable threat to the regime's predatory operations.

Under those circumstances it is easily foreseeable that, even long years after the government actions, Turkish society will likely bear deep scars from these events. After all, they happened in the full sight of people and, as far as I could observe, many people failed to approach victims with a basic human decency. Thus, the cumulative effects of the repressive violence has left its mark on the society as a whole, and people have become fearful about openly expressing their thoughts. Be that as it may, I believe there were even less defensible excuses than fear.

Whatsoever may be further observed on this, those who were dismissed stayed dismissed, those who were tortured stayed tortured, while large masses of poor and conservative voters, relying on his pretended promotion of piety, allowed Erdoğan to dominate the electoral arena and engage in predatory policies that ultimately will turn against them and have the effect to forfeit both national and private wealth. Islamist ideology of sub-urban constituencies thus found its way out of the Palace.

REGIME AND SOCIETY

Up to this point – and also in whole chapters of the book –, instead speaking of the "government," I have used the term "regime" as if this choice of terminology could be taken for granted, and I have occasionally referred to "Erdoğan" and the "Palace" – where he built all the offices as well as being resident therein – as if these pairs of terms were interchangeable. At first glance, endorsing the obvious signification of the word "regime" and its equivalence with the terms Erdoğan and Palace may seem an arguable proposition. However, as I am discussing at length in chapter 9, when the constitutional amendments approved by the referendum of 16 April 2017, and the presidential decrees issued subsequent to the 24 June elections of 2018 are carefully considered, I argue that it could be conceived that the term "regime" is not unsubstantiated. That is, a regime with some "electoral" components in which the ruler's power is exercised not over the territory, but the flock. Speaking in a Foucaultian terminology (Dean, 2013), such a situation is akin to the "shepherd-flock" game descended from the ancient Mesopotamian and Egyptian state formations.

A *second* oddity that can be traced throughout the following chapters in various contexts, however, is a "critique of society." I feel that, at this juncture, we need to use concepts that enable us – obviously without being pejorative – to put forward a critique of society, its institutions and practices, and even its ways of reasoning and forms of knowledge, in a methodical way. Thus, a critical reading can only reject the naturalisation of such corrupt concepts like the wholesale subordination to the will of rulers, the concentration of power in one hand, the mass dismissal or detention of people, dispossession through forfeiture, reversing of the burden of proof, running the economy through hot money, and so forth.

This critique primarily addresses the concepts and tools with which individuals of today think and transform the world. My main point is that, thinking with the mind-sets borrowed from those who are digging our grave, we are unlikely to find any exit from our predicament.

Further to this, as the victims of the regime, we should discover new paths of articulation and move to questioning the conditions under which we have been living by confronting the tradition which is built on imposing consent to the political/religious orders as if it was something equal to submission to God's plan.

I would never know how those involved in the regime could be able to claim access to God's plan, but such kind of interpretations seemed to me like a part of the Erdoğanist plan: intimidate and pacify enough of dissenting voices until they have lost their will or capacity to oppose the political development. In another sense, such a situation is also comparable to what Linda Weiss (1997: 193) calls the "political construction of helplessness", i. e. , telling citizens that they have no chance of control in the face of global trends.

Instead, I suggest, all of us, all the victims of the regime, should be much more than we are. Namely, rather than being simply dissenting people, relying on the availability of a great number of groups whom the State labelled as an "enemy of the nation and state," we could collectively translate dissenting communities of which we are part into "social movements."

C. Tilly (1998), a prominent political scientist, distinguishes social movements from ordinary interest groups with reference to their "collective claims on authorities." A social movement as a distinctive political phenomenon, Tilly suggests, "consists of a sustained challenge to power holders in the name of a population living under the jurisdiction of those power holders by means of repeated public displays of that population's numbers, commitment, unity, and worthiness".

The Gülen Movement, comprising the significant strata of society such as students, scholars, businessmen, workers, writers, civil servants, women's groups, and so forth, has been in the process of becoming a social movement. When operating under an oppressive political environment they learned to adjust their position in a way to defend fundamental rights, including freedom of expression and non-discrimination, and to advocate and praise pluralistic and democratic values. Inversely related to this trend, however, was a dramatic decline in public sympathy (on the right-wing), thereby sealing the correctness of the way. It was my observation that, through a centrally-organised public campaign, society was, in an alarmist mode, more oriented towards Gülen sympathizers as a danger than it had been against any other social movement.

However, the abortive coup of 15 July sharply disrupted this process. In that sense, the rise of the Gülen Movement, whether intentionally or not, to a form of social movement has remained an unfinished agenda in the hands of its followers, at least in Turkey of today. Yet it is the agenda that, I hope, the followers will turn to in the future. *(See figure 2, page 220)*

A *third* important issue is an inquiry into forms of interaction between Islam and Islamic extremism as represented by the personage of Erdoğan, of course, to some extent. In pursuing this approach, as the readers may perceive, I am making a clear distinction between *Islam* and *Islamism* in order to identify the responsible driver for returning Turkey to an authoritarian regime. In this sense, this book strongly suggests that Islamism acts as a destructive force against Islam itself (see chapter 7).

The main actors on stage were all Islamists endorsing the regime's authoritarian goals as well as the systematic exclusion of the Gülen community from Turkish social and economic life. Even though it still remains unknown what really impelled them to do so, the SoE period marked their disengagement from the community of civic peoples. And I believe this disengagement needs to be interrogated particularly by anthropologists and political scientists in the future.

Of course, it is an argument that Islamism and authoritarianism are intimately linked. But, from what we have observed in the last decade of politics in Turkey, while Islam as a religion strongly disapproves of arbitrary rule,[4] I suggest that Islamism as an ideology inevitably leads to authoritarian regimes where it is conflated with the *gastro-politic* engagements as well as the employment of both nationalist and religious discourses.

Over the years, I have increasingly become interested in contemporary efforts in "public anthropology" to bring interpretive sensitivity to the everyday character of human sociality. In this book, I also attempted to extend anthropological thinking to contemporary Turkish society, to the extent allowed by the context. So, as a non-academic writer, I believe such attention may provide a novel ground for exploring the roots of corruption in society and the body politic, on the one hand, as well as, on the other hand, religious intolerance expressing itself in ways that intertwine religion with ethnicity, hatred, and matters of state control.

---

4. Some recent research may shed light on this matter. For example, C. Boix (2003) finds that Islam has no effect on democratic transitions and is positively associated with democratic consolidation, while K. Meyer, D. Tope, and A. M. Price (2008) find that it is Islam, more than any other major religion, which promotes an individual-level support for democracy.

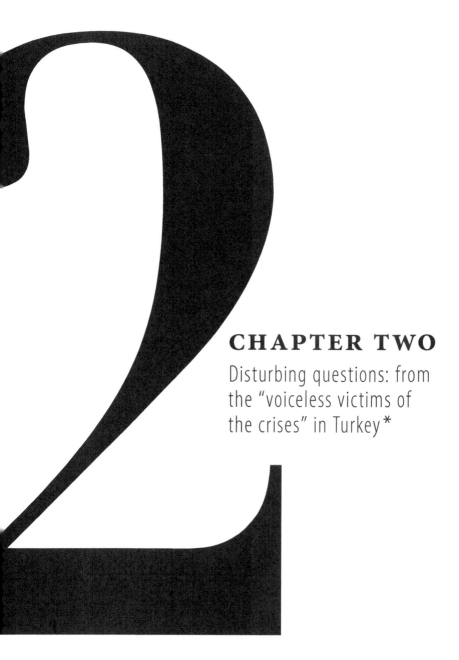

CHAPTER TWO

Disturbing questions: from the "voiceless victims of the crises" in Turkey*

* Initial version of this chapter first appeared as an article at the PPJ website on 11.7.2017.

> Nothing is more inconsistent than a political regime that is indifferent to the truth: but nothing is more dangerous than a political system that claims to prescribe the truth
>
> Michel Foucault

COUNTRY: TURKEY

In August of 2016, N. H. (27), a housewife from the Sinop province, was detained during the police control in traffic and put into the Sinop Prison. She was charged with the membership of the Gülen Movement because she allegedly had an encrypted messaging app. , *ByLock*,[1] on her mobile. N. H. was 14-week pregnant with twins and within 19 day of detention she lost her twins. Just after a two-day stay in hospital she was put back into jail. The case was quoted by prominent columnist Emin Çölaşan from the grieving husband's letter.[2]

In October 2016, a university teacher, Kam (34), was arrested in İzmir Province. She was detained for two months for investing *Bank Asya* (see chapter 5), an allegedly Gülen-affiliated bank. She was kept in a cell with her seven-month-old son and

---

1. The Erdoğan regime prosecutes the users of this smartphone app. with the accusation of being linked to the "Fethullahist Terror Organisation" although it was commercially available to download by anyone.
2. http://www. sozcu. com. tr/2016/yazarlar/emin-colasan/bu-haksizliklari-durdurun -1 448 641/(Accessed: 15 October 2016).

two other babies, where they were prohibited from crawling on the floor. Toys were also prohibited, and they didn't even have access to clean water.[3]

In March 2017, a pregnant woman whose husband had already been detained delivered a baby in solitude by herself when she was in detention in the Police Department of Ankara, without any medical support. She was then reluctantly hospitalized.[4]

In November 2018, a breastfeeding woman, Ayşe Ş. Taş, was arrested with the accusation of being affiliated to the Gülen Movement and, together with her 25-day baby, put into the prison of Ferizli, Sakarya. Worse still, witnesses say, she was rebuked by the judge for giving birth as such (Tutsak Bebekler, 2018).

In January 2017, policemen went into a hospital in Alanya of Antalya and were a little more tolerant. They kindly waited in front of the room before taking a pregnant woman who is being prosecuted. Right after the delivery, she was detained together with the new-born baby.[5]

In January 2017, a woman with 5 children (one with Down's syndrome) was detained in the entrance of the Sincan Prison of Ankara during their visit to the husband/father, and children were left alone screaming. The case recorded by a video shot by the eldest boy was reported by Mahmut Tanal, a prominent MP from the main opposition party, Republican People's Party (CHP).[6] *(See figure 3, page 221)*

---

3. http://www.foxnews.com/world/2018/02/13/hundreds-young-turkish-children (Accessed: 13 2. 2018).
4. http://siyasihaber3.org/hamile-kadin-hucrede-kendi-kendine-dogum-yapti (Accessed: 27 March 2017).
5. https://www.evrensel.net/haber/306 206/1-gunluk-bebegi-ile-gozaltina-alindi (Accessed: 31 1. 2017).
6. http://www.cumhuriyet.com.tr/haber/turkiye/664 494/Cezaevi_ziyaretinde_anneleri_de_gozaltina_alinan (Accessed: 23 1. 2017).

One common point in the stories of those people: they are the victims of the State who are probably never going back to having a normal life. They live in a world with a shared vulnerability to the state terror and violence. The stories I summarised above are about hundred thousands of real people, husbands, wives, and children, whose lives were torn apart by the violence and can never be made whole again.

MERCY VS. MERCILESSNESS

The cases above were selected among numerous arbitrary detentions by Turkish law enforcement bodies since the introduction of the SoE. In each of these cases, public prosecutors accused the women of being affiliated to the Gülen sympathisers, which Erdoğan has attributed the organisation of the coup attempt of 15 July 2016 to, but the international community has not been convinced so far. [1]

What is striking in this context is the explicit incompatibility of these practices with the Islamic rhetoric employed by the ruling Justice and Development Party (AKP). Erdoğan and his top guys refer to main religious merits such as justice, tolerance, mercy etc. , not only in the voting seasons but at every chance they get. In a country with an overwhelming Muslim majority that seems to be the norm if you wish to be perceived by voters as a "pious" man.

This can be better observed during the nation-wide ceremonies under the title of "Holy Birth Week" between 16 and 20 of April. Within these ceremonies led by the AKP government and its civil proponents, Prophet Mohammed (Peace be upon Him) is presented as "The Prophet sent as a mercy to the worlds." Muslims are rightly proud of Prophet Mohammed's merciful personality as it is the main constituent of the universe in Islamic rhetoric: "He [Allah] has prescribed Mercy on Himself" (Qur'an: Al-An'am, 12). Of course, there is no problem with the essence of this message.

However, increasing evidence implies that such messages were not really adopted or interpreted as limited to their own followers. It could even be said that, it is not mercy but *mercilessness* that has governed their mental image of the "National Will". Thus, in his public speeches, Erdoğan articulates this principle as the following: "If you keep showing mercy, at the end you will become the one to be shown mercy!"

Here, I would only point out that, in their understanding, females and children are not exempt from this principle; the standard of "guilt by association" applies in strict terms when their husband/father is deemed guilty. As OHCHR (2018) correctly put it, in almost all cases, the women were arrested as associates of their husbands, who were the regime's primary suspects for linkages to the Gülen Movement, without individual evidence supporting charges against them.

Far from it, for example, if a pregnant woman is poor she is dependent on the state for her survival. That is an essential of the "welfare state" founded upon a belief that the state bears responsibility to care for vulnerable citizens. Baby care behind bars is therefore a symptom of broader social and economic failures to care for society's most marginalised people (Sufrin, 2017).

FAMILIES UNDER THE "CIVIC DEATH" CONDITIONS

Since the failed coup, about 50.000 people have unjustly been jailed while more than 140.000 civil servants dismissed with lifelong banishment from public sector. When doing this, both Executive and Judicial powers interpreted the SoE regime in a way to overrule the fundamental rights protected by the Constitution as well as the ECHR.[7] This collaboration at the top triggered the pivotal process that I call the "crises". So, the term "state of emergency" does not and cannot explain the situation in Turkey.

Although arbitrary detentions and dismissals were criticised by the international community in various contexts, little attention has been devoted to the family members that were left behind. They even remained untouched by the speech held by Kemal Kılıçdaroğlu, the head of CHP, when the anti-Erdoğan "March for Justice" reached İstanbul on 9 July 2017.

They are also invisible to the public as purposely ignored by the mass media, ostracised by both society and state for the deeds of their parents and receive no benefits from social safety net from the government. Neither did Erdoğan accept to provide any financial redress (see the next chapter).

The term *Civic Death* (see chapter 4) suits best to their living conditions as the collective and sharp-edged character of the punishments made them devoid of regular income. That is the case especially for female-headed families. At present, those people seem to be more vulnerable than any Syrian immigrant in Turkey as the latter could survive with various forms of humanitarian assistance.

The international community should also be concerned that discriminative policy of Turkish government against those families would exacerbate the harshness of their subsistence and have a potential of exploitation and abuse. This pressing social issue may ultimately lead to a specific "humanitarian

---

7. http://www.echr.coe.int/Documents/Convention_ENG.pdf (Accessed: 10 July 2017).

action" unless necessary measures are taken by the regime in an appropriate and timely manner.

DEHUMANIZATION OF CHILDREN

In anthropological literature, there is an agreement that one of the universal norms in humans is "not to harm infants." That is even the norm among non-human primates. In many chimpanzee groups, harmful behaviour toward infants elicits particularly strong reactions such as interventions and defence of the mother-infant pair by multiple group members. This is called "third-party bystander reaction" (Burkart *et al.* 2018).

Likewise, human gatherings with a centrally organised polity give utmost importance to the safety of infants and pregnant women. The UN Convention on the Rights of the Child,[8] article 3(1) asks "the best interests of the child" to be a primary consideration in all actions concerning children, whether undertaken by public or private social welfare institutions, courts of law, administrative authorities or legislative bodies.

National legislations are also full of prohibitions imposing not harming infants. For example, in Turkey, the article 16(4) of Law no. 5275 concerning the execution of penalty and security measures[9] stipulates the deferral of execution of prison sentence for women who are pregnant or having a baby not older than 6 months.

Despite the clarity of these norms, it was reported by the Director General of the Prison and Detention Houses in a session held by the parliamentary Commission of Human Rights

---

8. https://www.ohchr.org/en/professionalinterest/pages/crc.aspx (Accessed: 6 August 2018).
9. Law no. 5275 was published in the Official Gazette of 29 December 2004, with no. 25 685.

that, as of November 2018, 743 mothers are behind bars together with their children-between 0 – 6 years old- while 35 women are pregnant.[10] <this has become the norm since the coup attempt in July 2016 which was refered to as *Dei Gratia* by Erdoğan and received less reaction from Turkish society.[11] A "third-party bystander reaction" then appears to be the last resort for them.

The fact that the majority of women and men in detention are parents of dependent children should lead politically sensitive bystanders like "Friends of Turkey" and human rights organisations to call on the regime in Turkey to take measures in order to promote social inclusion of these people. It is therefore worth asking a few questions to consider more carefully the current conditions in which the victims still live:

1. *Since 15 July of 2016, how many families have been affected by the coup-related detentions and dismissals?*

2. *How many families have experienced financial losses as a result of parental incarceration?*

3. *How many of them have been provided welfare assistance in either cash transfer or in-kind contribution, and how NGOs could involve existing governmental assistance programmes?*

4. *Are there any mechanisms that help families protect, nur-*

---

10. See, for example, the following link: https://ahvalnews.com/turkish-prisons/turkish-prisons-housing-40 000-over-capacity-says-prisons-director (Accessed: 19 11. 2018).
11. This drama was also reported by the Fox News in 13 2. 2018. See the following link: http://www.foxnews.com/world/2018/02/13/hundreds-young-turkish-children (Accessed: 6 August 2018).

ture and care for detainees' children? If no, what is the state of affairs in the field?

5. *Is there any mechanism providing or advocating for parenting programmes in prisons? If no, what is the state of affairs in the field?*

6. *Which kind of services and activities that assist detainees in carrying out family roles and responsibilities are in place?*

7. *Which types of measures has the government introduced to mitigate family crises, loss and demoralization, and victimization of children?*

8. *How many women have remained as single mothers who are assumed to be the sole care givers for their children?*

9. *How many parents have been prohibited from seeing their children at all because the children are under the custody of the child welfare department?*

10. *Has the government allocated additional human resources and/or budget to the Ministry of Labour, Family and Social Services in order to mitigate extra workload driven by the parental incarceration? If no, what is the state of affairs in the field?*

Finally, but not less relevant, within the context of parental incarceration, it should be interrogated whether special consideration is given to a "Child-Sensitive Social Protection" (UNICEF, 2012) aiming at reducing and eliminating the economic and social vulnerabilities of children, women and families in order to ensure their rights to a decent standard of living and essential services. *(See figure 4, page 221)*

The regime's spokesmen in Turkey frequently shares updated figures of detentions, arrests, and dismissals with the media to prove that there is progress in the struggle with "terrorists" i. e. dissent groups. Sure, that is a good communication policy that may encourage foot-dragging police chiefs to go witch-hunting. We could then be fully confident that those spokesmen would not have difficulty to respond the questions above.

We are also fully confident that, when any regime starts harming infants and women its agents fall below the morality of non-human primates. As J. Inda (2005) simply put it, one of the few legitimate ways for individuals to get access to social protection: that is, citizenship. But the regime in Turkey refuses some citizens the access to social protection when they are most in need.

SENSITIVITY TO THE SUFFERING OF "OTHERS"

Questions like those above make sense if you believe that everyone, whether he/she is guilty or not, just on the basis of being Human, has the right to live without inhuman or degrading treatment or punishment; without discrimination on any ground such as sex, race, colour, language, religion, political or other opinion, national or social origin, association with a national minority, property, birth or other status. Otherwise, they can disturb your ease.

Although this description is highly promoted by the international community, it would not be realistic for the victims to expect solidarity from the majority of the Muslim world including the Turkish society. Available evidence indicates that in this cultural niche of the world, "social polarisation" characterized by hatred, absolutism, and ideological rigidity does not leave any room to develop certain abilities of the human being such as the ability to think lucidly, the ability to communicate truthfully, and sensitivity to the suffering of "others". As Martín-Baró (1989) correctly identified, impoverishment of these human abilities just serves a process of dehumanization.

Therefore, it would be very significant if these questions were brought on the agenda of the European Parliament and/or national parliaments, included into the checklists of UN, EU commissioners in charge of human rights, taken place and followed up within the country reports of relevant organisations like Human Rights Watch, Amnesty International, Freedom House, Chatham House etc. mentioned and brought into attention by journalists, human rights activists in free media.

CONCLUSION: BEING THE VOICE OF VOICELESS

Even if it fails, every effort to carry the topics up to headlines means to be the "voice of voiceless" in the full sense of the word. On the contrary, sitting back implies that suffering people should be abandoned to their fates.

We asked no disturbing questions, but quoted extremely disturbing stories of pregnant women and babies in jail. Rather than blaming any political figure or government, they indict a cruel society that all but coerces women living on the margins of life far away from necessary medical and obstetric care.

Also, you may not hope that Turkish politicians are familiar with the concepts like parenting issues, family roles etc. Whatever the case may be, it is vital for a democratically elected government to be clear about the following: social and economic risks that directly affect women's and children's lives are to be taken as a "primary concern". That is what true mercy is!

CHAPTER THREE

Decree laws as means of the revival of the "civil death" in Turkey*

* Initial version of this chapter first appeared as an article at the PPJ website on 28.7.2017.

*In the story of David and Goliath,
hunger is David's stone.*

Sharman Apt Russell

HUNGER STRIKE

Nuriye G. (academic) and Semih Ö. (teacher) were just two of the victims fired because of the decree laws introduced under the SoE. Although it remains highly uncertain what they can achieve against an unconcerned government they went on a hunger strike to get their jobs back.

A Hunger strike, what Sharman Apt Russell (2005) identifies in her seminal book *Hunger: An Unnatural History* as "an established cultural form of seeking justice in the 20th Century", is generally preferred by those who are from the leftist tradition.

On the conservative side of the political divide, however, available evidence reveals that access to **food** and nutrition holds much more importance than hunger. As a person living in a conservative environment, I have often observed that the symbolic and the practical aspects of feeding are always in the mind of the conservative man as a religiously connoted act.

Therefore, it is normal to see that the followers of Erdoğan opposed the hunger strike in question with some religious arguments.[1]

But the court in Ankara did more than this: Nuriye and Semih, were detained on 23 May 2017, the 76th day of their strike, with the following justification: "in case they are not arrested, they could harm the operability of the justice!" Such reasoning was likely the first in judicial history of Turkey.[2]

Nuriye and Semih decisively continued the hunger strike in prison.[3] Unless any good progress happens, they likely will die at the end. Interestingly, that seems to be what Erdoğan really wants to see. His latest interviews with both national and foreign media gives some clue of his firm stance against such victims of the SoE. *(See figure 5, page 222)*

"HOW COULD THERE BE SUCH AN APPROACH?"

In an exclusive interview with BBC World in 14th of July 2017,[4] Zainab Badawi asked Turkish President Erdoğan about nearly 200.000 Turkish citizens who are detained, sacked or suspended from their jobs following the failed coup.

How are they going to survive if they've lost their jobs? They also have dependents; they have elderly relatives, children [...] Does the Turkish government provide them with social security payments? Because they have been stripped of their livelihoods. What happens to their families if they can't work again?

By the way, as a fine coincidence, Zainab Badawi had for-

---

1. See, for example: http://www.bbc.com/turkce/39 974 008 (Accessed: 19 May 2017).
2. https://www.bbc.com/turkce/haberler-turkiye-40 006 978 (Accessed: 23 May 2017).
3. Court finally released Nuriye and Semih on 1 December 2017. They ended their hunger strike on 26 1. 2018 upon the refusal of their application for remitter by the Commission.
4. https://www.bbc.co.uk/programmes/p058hofs (Accessed: 23 May 2017).

mulated our recent "Disturbing Questions" (see chapter 2) into one genius question indeed.

Erdoğan replied with a mocking tone: *"For God's sake! How could there be such an approach? [...] The state does not have to look after everyone forever. Because these people are members of a terrorist organisation. Why should the state feed those who are members of a terrorist organisation?"* (emphasis added).

No surprise. If we translate these words, Erdoğan means to say: "we intend to kill them all, but you ask how they would survive!" His speeches on several occasions also prove this hatred: "we are going to behead these traitors [...] if parliament passes a bill on resuming executions, I sign it."[5]

Without going into deep semiotic interpretations, this kind of communication through metaphors of food/feeding involves a *gastro-political*[6] suggestion fully coherent with the primary concern that governs preferences of the conservative voters currently backing Erdoğan. In his *patriarchal* understanding, centrally-controlled resources represent a kind of "feeding capacity" so that the ruler can create "dependants" who are more than simple followers, for his own long-run purposes. This also explains why those women and children are not seen as worth feeding.

Strikingly, this dates back to the 24th century B. C. in the first great experiment with larger state formation in the Near East, that of Sargon of Akkad: "5.400 men daily eat in the presence of Sargon, the king to whom the god Enlil gave no rival", D. Frayne (1999: 29) quotes from a cuneiform inscription. Here, the power of the ruler is epitomized concretely by his authority and capability to extract staple resources from the realm and

---

5. See, for example: https://edition.cnn.com/2017/07/15/europe/turkey-coup-attempt-anniversary/index.html (Accessed: 16 July 2017).
6. The term *gastro-politics* refers to a political realm where food is the medium, and sometimes the message, of conflict. For further information, see Appadurai (1981).

so feed his own loyal administrators, priests, soldiers, servants, and so on. In ancient Mesopotamia, state-making was being performed, to a large extent, in the realm of gastro-politics.

By the same token, Erdoğan perceives – for example – payments in the form of salary or wage as instruments to affirm the connections between the ruler and those people whose role was to protect him and ensure the safety of his reign. From this vantage point, such payments are to feed public workers and they, in turn, should pay it back as loyalty to the regime. Those who fail to do so, however, lose the right to be paid as Erdoğan emphasised during the above-mentioned interview.

However, the more frightening point in this context is his pure "sincerity" in these words. This sharp tone at the top has played a decisive role in influencing public opinion to adopt the present silence above which the mass detentions and dismissals have raised. Children are likely to live in poverty if their parents are not employed or assisted financially. And against this, the President of the country recklessly argues that the state does not have to "feed" everyone forever.

Modern anthropology tells us "sensitivity to the suffering of others" takes its roots from the cultural evolution of our human ancestors. But as with Erdoğan and his top guys, increasing evidence has shown that there is no guarantee that social sufferings will be honoured by them.

Rather, thanks to the failed coup of 15 July 2016, instead of the death penalty, they seem to introduce an *ancient* status which already disappeared, "civil death". Possibly, taking the reactions of the international community into consideration, Erdoğan regime preferred this option through decree laws and arbitrary detentions.

CIVIL DEATH STATUS RE-EMERGED

Civil death or *civiliter mortuus* in Latin refers to the loss of all civil rights by a person tat has been sentenced to death or declared an outlaw for committing a felony or treason. An individual subjected to civil death forfeits his or her civil rights, including the ability to marry, the ability to own property, the right to contract, the right to sue, and the right to protection under the law (Saunders, 1970).

Punishing crime through limiting citizenship is a practice with deep roots in western society including ancient Greece and Roman worlds, then Medieval Europe. This kind of punishment suggests that, when convicted of certain crimes one would suffer "civil death", or the loss of all civil rights. Also, those criminals who were declared "outlaws" could be killed without penalty since they were literally considered to be "outside of the law". These punishments were viewed as so severe that they were reserved for only the most heinous of offenses (Miller and Spillane, 2012).

Being civically dead or remaining out of the law's protection, from a philosophical vantage, may entail a kind of "sacredness". G. Agamben (1998), with reference to archaic Roman law, describes *Homo sacer* as "the one whom the people have judged on account of a crime. It is not permitted to sacrifice this man, yet he who kills him will not be condemned for homicide." Indeed, this is a man who is put under the civil death conditions. Because Homo sacer is outside the purview of divine law, and because one who kills him cannot be accused of homicide, he is also outside the purview of human law.

Das and Poole (2004), following Agamben's analysis, suggest that law produces certain bodies as "killable" because they are positioned by the law itself as prior to the institution of law so that sovereign power could resort to a boundless state of exception.

In a nutshell, civil death extinguishes most civil rights of a person convicted of a crime and largely puts that person outside the law's protection.

From the literature, we also know that civil death as an institution faded away in the middle of the twentieth century. At least, it no longer exists under that name (Chin, 2012). Today, a democratic state ought to protect the civil rights of groups seeking unusual, unpopular, and even antisocial ends and rely on the protections afforded by constitutional processes to mitigate any harm that might accrue to society.

However, in today's Turkey, under the SoE conditions, effectually a new civil death is meted out to citizens accused of crimes in the form of a substantial and permanent change in legal status, operationalized by decree laws and some administrative restrictions, not by judicial decisions that being the most appropriate safeguard against arbitrariness.

As Semelin (2007) simply put it, when civil death is organised politically it becomes a rational means to an end: *genocide*. The following list of disenfranchisements that we summarised from the decree laws is to serve such an end in Turkey.

On the basis of the standard allegation i. e. "belonging to or being affiliated or connected to terrorist organisations or to organisations, entities or groups which the National Security Council (MGK) had found to be engaged in activities harmful to the State", all decree laws concerning dismissal stipulate that the civil servants in the annexed list are subject to;

1. **Dismissal from their duties in the public service without any further procedure to apply:** *with no judicial*

conviction or administrative proceeding, in one night, they lost their main source of substitution, monthly salary, which is vital for fulfilment of parental responsibilities.

2. **Lifelong prohibition to be reinstated:** *no chance to turn back, lifelong debarment applies.*

3. **Lifelong prohibition to be employed in the public service even in indirect ways:** *lifelong debarment from "public services", a term of which the scope is much wider than official duties in Turkish legal framework.*

4. **Withdrawal of the ranks and/or assignments without any criminal conviction:** *if you were a four-star general in the army, subsequent to dismissal you would be just a "private soldier" in military terms.*

5. **Cancellation of passports:** *a dismissed person is not allowed to go abroad, for example, to seek job opportunities. In other words, they are denied mobility, denied any exit from their predicament. That is also the case for his/her spouse.[7] A typical example of "guilt by association!" Therefore, as can be seen from the mass media, only illegal ways remain to be attempted: crossing the Aegean Sea or the river Evros (Maritza) by boats as asylum seekers fleeing economic hardship and genocide usually do.*

---

7. Article 10(2) of Decree Law no. 673 dated 1 September 2016 allows the Ministry of Interior to cancel the passports belonging to spouses if deemed risky for the general security. Yet the ministry announced the removal of the restriction on 25 July 2018 for those who had not been prosecuted but disabled because of prosecution against their spouses. The Ministry says 155.350 citizens in total would enjoy this removal. See: https://www.icisleri.gov.tr/pasaport-serhlerinin-kaldirilmasina-iliskin-duyuru (Accessed: 5 August 2018).

6. **Forfeiture of registered guns provided by the state:** *in Turkey, as a special kind of protection, certain sensitive post holders like judges, prosecutors, auditors etc. are provided low-price pistols against possible assaults during their duty. Forfeiture therefore implies that the vulnerability of these people will no longer be a matter of concern for the state.*

7. **Annulation of occupational licenses and rights:** *if you were a teacher in any public or private school, your formal license would be null and void subsequent to dismissal. That is also the case for other licensed professions such as lawyers, certified public accountants, pilots, captains etc.*

8. **Further sanctions imposed by the special laws:** *dismissal is to pave the way for civil death. It is followed by a series of sanctions from travel restrictions and detentions to arrest warrants as well as administrative precautions to prevent you of starting your own business or to deter employers of hiring you in their business.*

9. **No formal notice required:** *as you are regarded legally "dead", delivery of an official notice concerning your dismissal would be waste of paper.*

10. **No access to the surveillance files:** *if you wish to learn the reasons behind your dismissal and/or investigation, your petition remains unanswered because the resolution by the "Board of Assessment for Right to Information"*[8]

---

8. The Resolution can be seen from the following link: http://www.bedk.gov.tr/kurul-il-ke-kararlari.aspx (Accessed: 6 August 2018).

> says it falls under the articles 16, 19, and 20 of the Access to Information Law no. 4982, i. e. state security, investigation security, and judicial security. As for the post-SoE era, article 10 of Law no. 7145 dated 31 July 2018 moved the National Intelligence (MİT), leading force behind the blacklisting services in public, out of the scope of Law no. 4982. No right to access information in this matter.

> 11. **No religious burial service:** *as is known, mortuary rituals underpinning human religiosity carry an outsize importance in sociality of human beings. Concerning the citizens killed during the coup-related conflicts and identified by the authorities as a "coup plotter", the chairmanship of the Religious Affairs (Diyanet), however, declared that their corpses are not given religious services like salâ (proper announcement of death from the minarets) shrouding, and praying by imams.⁹ Fulfilment of these Islamic burial rituals therefore rests with their relatives.*

Worse still, together with the mentioned sanctions, the name-surname, position, and institution of the dismissed person appears on the internet-access Official Gazette.¹⁰ This publicity ensures that you would then be recognized by others as the government identifies, i. e. a "terrorist" or "traitor". Thus, for example, employers can legally refuse to hire you.

On the other hand, according to legal framework governing the social security system, when 100 days expired as from the date of dismissal, Social Security Institution will no longer pay for health services of those people and their family members.

---

9. 19th July 2016 dated Press Release of the Religious Affairs: http://www. aljazeera.com.tr/haber/darbecilerin-cenaze-namazi-kilinmayacak (Accessed: 6 August 2018).
10. See, for example, article 2 of the Decree Law no. 672 published in the Official Gazette of 1 September 2016, with no. 29 818 (2nd M).

This means that the "safety net" will not cover them and they are required to pay for it. In common usage, a safety net denotes the provision of services for disenfranchised people who need help meeting their basic needs and who would otherwise "slip through the cracks." As a social institution, the safety net represents a contested moral and ethical stance toward society's most vulnerable (Sufrin, 2017).

Here is the stance: the digitalized state operates against them in the public sphere from hospitals to notaries. From the regime's point of view, the most impressive way seems to be paved to send those "traitors" to hell as a warning to others.

Thus, on every occasion in the public arena from hospitals to notaries, you would face the fact of your dismissal. Publicity of your dismissal also ensures that you would not only suffer the insult of cover-ups and lies but you would often become target for harassment and abuse from the public officers, policemen, *imams*, neighbours, even from ordinary man in the street. Namely, the above listed "legal" stigmas were not independent with the everyday life.

Finally, but no less relevant, degradation of the individual's legal status by the regime left its marks on the human relations too. We know the consequences of being dismissed or detained have become worse for many Gülen sympathisers: many have been severely ostracised by even their closest relatives in the sense that no one speaks to them literally, or cooperate with them economically. If you have been dismissed from the public, your spouse has been arrested, or your economic assets have been forfeited, your very means of livelihood are in danger of being destroyed.

When it comes to your original legal status, it is in effect regarded as "dead" by the law anymore. That is the situation to which the civil death status refers in the *Medieval* doctrine. In short, you are treated as if already dead (Beety *et al.* 2015).

NO NEED TO "BEHEAD THESE TRAITORS"

In Turkey, a person dismissed or detained on suspicion of being linked to the "harmful" movements like Gülen, Kurdish, Marxist and so on, may be subjected to the restrictions above including the ineligibility to work in a particular occupation or even the ineligibility to establish or maintain family relations. This form of civil death seems to be more cost-effective than killing all them in the full sight of the world.

More than that, unlike a death penalty which destroys one's physical existence, civil death destroys the legal capacity of individuals forcing them into permanent exclusion from the civic order. Apart from other consequences, such discriminatory sanctions obviously degrade the meaning of citizenship for them. The term "variegated citizenship," referring to the conditions under which "some subjects are nurtured and afforded rights and resources while others are largely neglected or deprived of sustenance to survive" (Inda, 2005), better describes the new form of citizenship Erdoğan regime deems Gülen sympathisers worthy of.

What I would like to underline here is that the majority of people who have been accused of treason are not currently in prison. However, because of their dissenting positions recorded (!) by MİT, they remain subject to governmental intervention of various aspects of their lives and concomitant imposition of benefits and burdens. Accusation of involvement the coup attempt, however, remains a sham allegation to facilitate social stigma.

In those circumstances, it is normal to observe that some choose not to hire, rent or marry a person with a criminal label. The case of Turkey shows that "civic exclusion" of dissenters is better ensured in that way.

On the other hand, in both ancient and modern forms of civil death, disenfranchisement applies on the basis that a civil disability automatically follows a criminal sanction since a convicted prisoner will, for the duration of his sentence, lose certain rights. If he/she is convicted by the court with some disabilities going beyond prison, according to the laws on criminal record, when a certain period (3 years in Turkey)[11] as from the execution of the punishment expired, "expungement" procedure would apply upon request.

As for the case of Turkey, relying on the SoE, government devised civil death as a punishment associated with allegation (not conviction) for treason or felony.

Civil death in its original application was a transitional status in the period between a capital sentence and its execution, not a condition potentially applicable for decades (Chin, 2012). But in the lack of any judicial and/or administrative proceeding, dismissals including civil disabilities are put into force by the Palatial regime on a "lifelong" basis. This is followed by a nonstop campaign of stigmatization waged by pro-Erdoğan media.

Thus the loss of legal status is achieved through a multitude of governmental and social sanctions. I am referring to this entirety as a "revival of the civil death." Of course, honour (!) of its revival in the form of "a set of disenfranchisements imposed by decree laws based on the blacklisting" belongs to Erdoğan's "New Turkey".

---

11. For expungement procedure in Turkey, see article 13(A) of Law no. 5352 concerning the Criminal Records.

BLACKLISTING LEGALISED: CATALOGUING BY STATE AGENTS

Within the context of mass dismissals of the public officials in Turkey, civil death conditions were prepared through blacklisting (*"Fişleme"* in Turkish intelligence vocabulary), a secret process in which agents mainly from the public institutions, MİT, police and gendarmerie services, and – when relevant – civilians who gathered information and intelligence on anyone who steps out of line were involved.

Information gathering activities with a focus on specific orientations of the public officials in political, social, religious, sexual etc. sense are roughly described as blacklisting or cataloguing. Blacklisting also involves relatives and friends whom you are associated with and may judge you as a criminal because of this biological or social association. AYM, in its 4 August 2016 dated decision, calls intelligence gathered in that way as "social environment information" and grants a kind of legality in dismissals (see chapter 2). The latter is known as "guilt by association" in the literature.

The origin of blacklisting and the notion of guilt by association traces back to the second century A. D. , early Christian pundits who produced some catalogues branding "heretics" as Jews or pagans. Geoffrey S. Smith (2015), in his seminal book on the *Medieval* origins of cataloguing, suggests that Justin Martyr of Rome, an early Christian philosopher, was the first in cataloguing of the heretics. In his book written A. D. 147 – 154, "First Apology," Justin Martyr opens a special chapter: "Syntagma against All the Heresies" listing the heretical teachers, preachers, apostles, and groups etc. of the time.

Cataloguers tended to avoid direct confrontation with their opponents and instead preferred to discredit them behind their backs. From the tone and content of the cataloguing samples, it is inferred that, if you are *in the catalogue* you should be out of the community because you pose a threat to the integrity of the community. This catalogues thus provided the Church a powerful weapon to combat its gnostic opponents (Smith, 2015).

The sum total of blacklisting signals whether you may pose a threat to the regime. No time is spent in determining whether the target person is actually guilty of any crime; mere affiliation or association is sufficient to issue a *fiche* specific to you. As such, it differs from the "screening," a formal procedure carried out by the security services over track records of those who are candidate to sensitive posts in public institutions.

Nevertheless, do not expect this threat to be substantial or close to happening. Threat is assumed not by actions but "associations" and is assigned to all those who share the defining ascriptive characteristics. Let us take the story of V. Gordon Childe (1892–1957), most influential thinker in the history of archaeology, whose seminal book, "What Happened in History," is known to many of us. Yet recently released files kept by MI5, the British intelligence service, revealed that Childe had been catalogued as a committed Marxist and intensely surveilled until his death. Most importantly, pro-provost of Queens College Oxford he served at that time, openly accusing Childe of homosexuality, provided "information" to MI5 (Lever, 2015). This sample may give an insight into ultimate limits cataloguing can extend to.

Before and during the SoE regime in Turkey, blacklists were used in the establishment of rhetorically constructed groups of opponents, Gülen sympathisers in particular. It is known that mass dismissals and even non-trial detentions were based on the blacklists prepared in advance. Many civil servants were listed as being a member of the Gülen Movement. They were given no opportunity to challenge what was said about them and no opportunity to take themselves off it as blacklisting is done in secret.

One of the major problems arisen from the blacklisting is its informal character which is lacking any legal ground. As such, blacklists cannot be valued as evidence before the courts. To tackle this problem at least in military context, with the article 41 of the Decree Law no. 694 dated 25 8. 2017, MİT was tasked with the "cataloguing" of military staff working at the central and provincial organisations of the Ministry of National Defence and its affiliated institutions (i. e. General Staff, Commanderships of the Air, Naval, and Land Forces, military schools, and National Defence University) in order to assess whether they may pose a threat to the regime.

To this end, MİT gets access to all public documentation and is authorised to every kind of investigation inside and outside institutions including military facilities. MİT thus becomes a specialized institution of the regime as the last word in recruitment, promotion, and dismissal of the military staff.

As can be understood, the provision concerned grants a kind of "legality" to the blacklisting by MİT. This may lead to direct acceptance of the "evidences" yielded from blacklisting in a judicial sense, as well implying the illegality of the previous ones.

Lastly, blacklisting also functions as a reference in production of the institutional "opinion" *(kanaat)* with respect to the dismissal of the target person. Dismissal by decree law, however, provides a plausible deniability of institutional involvement in the process: we did not initiate your dismissal in any way, but the decree law issued by the Cabinet.

Yet article 12(4) of the "Working Procedures and Principles of the SoE Inquiry Commission"[12] requires the institutions involving blacklisting to share their opinion and relevant intelligence documentation with the Commission in its review of appeals. Thus, blacklist-based opinions are granted a kind of legal base to proceed this self-evidencing mechanism assuming that anyone who challenges the regime, in one way or another, cannot be employed in public services.

CONCLUSION

Under the leadership of Erdoğan, Turkey is heading towards an increasingly dangerous situation in which civil death could become a reality for some victims. The victims of the SoE, sooner or later, may face this reality as long as the international community remains mere bystander and fails to show active solidarity with them.

---

12. Relying on the article 13 of the Decree Law no. 685, PM Circular concerning the "Working Procedures and Principles of the SoE Inquiry Commission" was published in the Official Gazette of 12 July 2017, with no. 30 122 (M).

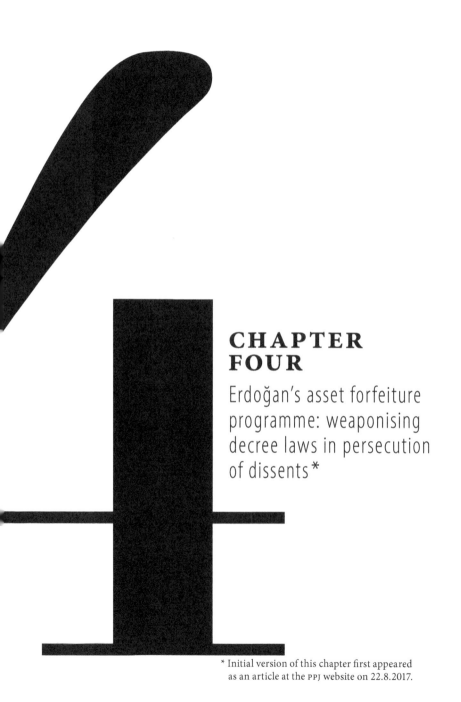

CHAPTER FOUR

Erdoğan's asset forfeiture programme: weaponising decree laws in persecution of dissents*

* Initial version of this chapter first appeared as an article at the PPJ website on 22.8.2017.

> He [Christ] said to them, "it is written,
> 'my house shall be called a house of prayer'
> but you make it a den of robbers.
> Matthew (21:13)"

DESPOTIC GOVERNMENT

In his *PERSIAN LETTERS*, MONTESQUIEU (2008), by comparing East and West from the observations of fictional oriental travellers, describes "despotic government" as a government that is entirely in the hands of a single man who is the sovereign chief both in spiritual as well as in worldly affairs; the complete master of the life and goods of his subjects.

Yet Montesquieu does not give special consideration to the situation of public/private goods in view of the forfeiting capacity of such a government in the sense of property rights, likely because of less historical evidence in his days. Or possibly, he remained under the sway of "horror, darkness, and terror", distinctive features of despotic governments as represented by the oppressive monarchy of France at those times.

Whatsoever, if Montesquieu lived in today's world, he would likely see that the evidence does not come from the East only, but mostly from the post-colonial governments of twentieth century. He would easily identify the Duvaliers in Haiti, the Somozas in Nicaragua, Amin in Uganda, Bokossa in the Central

African Republic, and Marcos in the Philippines as non-exhaustive examples of the well-known rulers who all deserve the epithet of kleptocrats. Nevertheless, with the fall of Mobutu of Zaire in 1997, as many of us, Montesquieu could also assume that such rulers' reign would once come to an end.

Contrary to what is assumed, the happenings in Turkey subsequent to the "December 2013" scandals[1] concerning widespread corruption at the top have made clear that a despotic type of government never disappears. Further, we have seen that it may even maintain itself in an electoral democracy. Having crowded by general, presidential and local elections, and referenda each of which the winner is always the same, Erdoğan, the last decade of Turkey provides a good evidence of this argument.

Today, Erdoğan is the President of the Republic, and at the same time, the head of the ruling party, AKP. Although, in all public speeches, he uses a language that could be considered uncivil, he receives positive responses from the majority of voters. That was almost the case in every voting season.

Thus, with reference to the present conditions of Turkey, we could fill in the page Montesquieu left blanked. This page suggests that if an autocrat wishes to sleep in peace, he should promote a war of extermination that continues to be waged between incumbent and dissents until the latter becomes extinct. Hence, the "asset forfeiture programme" finds its real value within that notion.

FORFEITURE IN A NUTSHELL

Authors are used to explaining the term "forfeiture" with reference to the Biblical passage: *"if an ox gores a man or a*

---

1. For a brief summary: https://en.wikipedia.org/wiki/2013_corruption (Accessed: 20 8. 2017).

woman, that they die, the ox shall be surely stoned, and its flesh shall not be eaten." The medieval notion of "deodand" which is derived from the Latin phrase "Deo Dandum" meaning "to be given to God" can also be seen as an archaic form of civil forfeiture. In both origins, forfeiture was initially confined to "guilty property". However, it was later expanded to include all property and chattels belonging to criminals, serving, in principle, as a type of fine (Schwarcz and Rothman, 1993).

In its ancient forms, asset forfeiture was mainly used by governments to fight piracy. Simply, if the government forfeits the ship used in piracy instead of jailing the crew only, this prevents the criminal activity from continuing. More recently, forfeiture has emerged as a powerful tactical weapon in the fight against organised crime and drug trafficking (Dery, 2012).

As for the term "confiscation," it is a penalty or a measure ordered by a court following proceedings in relation to a criminal offence resulting in the final deprivation of property. Forfeiture is also synonymous with confiscation in both civil and criminal procedures, particularly when it refers to the removal of direct advantages (European Commission, 2009).

In brief, asset forfeiture involves government seizure of the personal assets obtained from or used in a crime. Otherwise, such needs to be called as robbery or plunder in legal sense.

FORFEITURE IN TURKEY: A BRIEF HISTORY

Historical background of the concept leads us to suggest that, in modern Turkey, forced transfer of property from Christian into Muslim-Turk hands *(Turkification)* at the end of the Greek-Turkish war (1920 – 22) by the commissions in charge of confiscating, registering, and selling movable and immovable "abandoned properties" *(emval-i metruke)* was the first in that sense (Morack, 2018).

Yet the "Capital Tax" of 1942 putting the assets of certain taxpayers into an arbitrary assessment and ultimate forfeiture by the government is the most studied case both in home and abroad. Available evidence indicates that the law on the capital tax was purposely designed in a way to lead the government to forfeit the wealth gathered in the hands of non-Muslim citizens. Or, alternatively they were forced to give up their properties with less worthwhile prices. Needless to say, the huge majority of buyers were emerging Turkish merchants.

The implementation of Law no. 4305 concerning the Capital Tax[2] was thus based on the division of taxpayers into two main categories: M (Muslim) and G (Gayrımüslim: Non-Muslim). Later two more categories were added: E (Ecnebi) for foreigners and D (Dönme) for the members of the Sebataist sect of Jewish "converts" to Islam (Angeletopoulos, 2008).

From the government's point of view, citizens in category G and D had made extraordinary profits during the turmoil of World War II (WWII) and this should have been levied. To this end, the law required taxpayers to pay the allocated tax "in cash" within a fortnight. More strikingly, assessments were "final" and there was no administrative or judicial remedy to exhaust.

Against excessive tax burden beyond their paying capacity, many sold their properties for a song while forfeiture procedure applied for real estates. Those who failed to pay were deported to Aşkale, near the Erzurum province in the eastern part of Turkey, where they would engage in road construction until their debts were fully paid. Out of 40.000 tax debtors, about

---

2. Law no. 4305 was published in the Official Gazette of 12 11. 1942, with no. 5255.

5.000 were sent to the camps in Aşkale, and all of these were members of non-Muslim communities.

Wealth tax was withdrawn in March 1944 under the pressure of criticism from Britain and the United States (İnce, 2012).

Apart from this intervention of the one-party regime ruling under the WW II conditions, over the course of Turkey history, asset forfeiture largely remained, as it was generally the case in Western countries, limited to fight against organised crimes like smuggling, money laundering, drug trafficking, etc.

FORFEITURE IN THE REIGN OF ERDOĞAN

Although asset forfeiture exists almost in all countries, the cruelty of Erdoğan's asset forfeiture program is something that Turkish society had never witnessed. That is the case both in terms of asset size and of numbers of citizens affected.

Indeed, this attack launched by the government was not a midnight operation facilitated by the coup attempt of last year only. It was a cumulative impact of power grabs that have been achieved by the ruling party, AKP in the political realm. To understand how it works, let us bear in mind that the AKP has its roots in the *Islamist* movement: "National Outlook" *(Milli Görüş)*.[3] First and foremost, the distinctive trait of this movement is that the power is highly concentrated in the hands of one single individual. It is therefore not a surprise that Islamist movements are being represented by "hegemonic" parties in the political realm. The AKP is also a good example of this kind in Turkey.

---

3. For a brief analyse of the interactions between AKP and National Outlook, see Yılmaz (2017).

Hegemonic parties require mass support to survive when they rise to power. Because of this, from the time he was new in the office, Erdoğan has employed main sources of the country as *gastro-political instruments* to create a market for political loyalty to make citizens vest their interests in the survival of the existing government. This policy not only made his power more secure, but also paved the way for the punishment of potential opponents with impunity.

Parallel to this, as the AKP has become more capable of creating an image of invincibility that will discourage potential challengers, it devoted its power to change the constitution to erect autocratic electoral entities such as the AYM, high courts, the HSK or the Grand National Assembly (TBMM). Not only the mass support of voters in the referendum of 16 April 2017, but also the facts that;

a. *one of the opposing parties opted to survive as a "satellite" organisation of the AKP,*

b. *another positioned itself as "loyal opposition,", considering itself being better off.*

played a key role in achieving the constitutional changes towards a one-man rule in the form of the so-called Executive Presidency.

Given the circumstances and the actors at play, we should not be surprised if less reaction was heard when the asset forfeiture programme started. And we should have known what would happen with the expansion of forfeiture powers.

DECREE LAWS AS A MEANS OF FORFEITURE

Since the coup attempt of 15 July 2016, asset forfeiture has become one of the greatest threats to property rights and due process in Turkey. Taking advantages of the SoE regime, the government introduced a large-scale forfeiture programme through decree laws. The target was economic capability of citizens who are seen linked with the *Gülen Movement, the* alleged plotter of the coup.

Erdoğan's forfeiture programme mainly works in two ways: (1) some assets, as it was the case in expropriation, are handed over directly to relevant public institutions by the new formal owner, the Ministry of Treasury and Finance, while (2) some are managed by an appointed "trustee" at first hand and ultimately sold to private tenderers. The type and function of the assets are taken into consideration in this division.

Here is the point: in both categories, forfeiture serves to draw resources from the economic to the political sphere where the "corporate titans" gather, holding resources so as to obtain rents instead of producing goods and services. It is out of question that this political sphere expanded, becoming increasingly invasive and in the end coincided with the interests of the Palatial regime and its affiliates, above all based initially on an ideological consensus, derived from a powerful religious legitimation and probably also thanks to the common perception of the merits (!) of the "Directly Unproductive Profit-seeking" (DUP) activities for long-term political goals.[4]

---

4. Bhagwati *et al.* (1984) appear to be the first formally analysing individual DUP phenomena (e. g. revenue seeking, tariff seeking, monopoly seeking, etc.) as the "ways of making a profit (i. e. income) by undertaking activities which are directly unproductive; that is, they yield pecuniary returns but produce neither goods and services that enter a conventional utility function directly nor intermediate inputs into such goods and services."

Direct Forfeiture: Just after the failed coup, Decree Law no. 667 was introduced on 23 July 2016. By the article 2(1) of the Decree, 4.911 private assets in total were forfeited together with the removable items like furniture, office and IT equipment, broadcasting and printing machines, medical devices, etc. (Table 1).

Table 1: Forfeited Assets by Type and Numbers (2016 – 2017)

Assets Forfeited	Total # of Assets
Private hospital	40
Association, foundation, and their economic facilities	1.406
University and affiliated hospital (15+7)	22
Syndicate, fedaration, and confederation	51
Schools and courses (1135+1078)	2.213
Dormitory and boarding house	1.005
Radio and TV Channels	69
Newspaper, periodical, publish house, news agency	105
Total	4.911

Data Source: Annual Activity Report by the DG National Estates (2017)

The entities which were lawful organisations were permanently closed and activities ended because of alleged ties to the Gülen Movement. It is unknown whether any assessment – in terms of due diligence – was made for their assets. It is also unknown to us how much money was forfeited at the deposit accounts held by these entities.

Later, 146 media outlets in total were added into the list above by Decree Law no. 668 (27 July 2016) and Decree Law no. 675 (29 October 2016). However, in line with the article 20(3) of Decree Law no. 674 (1 September 2016), some components of this latter group were handed over by the Ministry of Treasury and Finance to the Savings Deposit Insurance Fund (TMSF) for sale. A Huge amount of high-tech broadcasting equipment was effective in this transfer.

Decree laws concerned, within their standardised article 2(2), stipulate that all kinds of assets belonging to those entities are to be transferred to the Treasury (The National Estates) with no charge and real estates registered automatically on behalf of the Treasury. the transfer process is managed by the Ministry of Treasury and Finance and the General Directorate of Foundations.

In principle, such forfeiture requires the prosecutors to obtain a criminal conviction. Simply stated, it is the seizure of property derived from a crime, involved in a crime, or which makes a crime easier to commit or harder to detect. In direct forfeitures, however, having ties to the Gülen Movement is considered as a criminal activity involving the coup attempt despite lack of any causality between the coup and the forfeited assets. No prosecutor, no judge, to proceed in due process!

Decree laws also indicate that direct forfeiture is not limited to the mentioned assets but is legal in case of "liabilities", too. For example, if you were a teacher who is working at one of those schools on the date of shutting down you would get neither any remaining salary nor damages. Further, if you were a parent who made an advance payment to the school to which your child was attending, you would never get this money back. When it comes to "receivables", no exemption, debtors should pay it to the new "owner" of the school!

Yet, on 17 8. 2016, article 5 of the Decree Law no. 670 recognized such liabilities to be released upon submission of documentary proof unless the claimants are linked with the Gülen Movement. However, in practice, for example, someone who preferred Gülen-inspired schools is treated as a follower of the movement.

On the other hand, Erdoğan's forfeiture programme is not limited to the private assets in Turkey only and tends to go beyond the national boundaries when possible. As is known, right after the failed coup of 15 July 2016, Erdoğan called on all countries to close the schools and other educational centres tied to the Gülen Movement which he has dubbed "FETÖ," an acronym for Fethullahist Terror Organisation.

To this end, the "Turkish Education Foundation" *(Türkiye Maarif Vakfı* – TMV*)* was established by Law no. 6721 on 28 June 2016.[5] TMV is to be financed from the national budget and staff be granted diplomatic immunity to facilitate abroad operations against the schools considered tied to the Gülen Movement. Lastly, by the Cabinet Decree no.2018/11 995, 351 million Turkish Liras (TL), appr. $70 million at that time, was transferred from the Ministry of National Education to the TMV's bank account on 24 June 2018, i. e. Election Day![6]

"Quick expropriation" of real estates is another way of direct forfeiture that has increasingly been applied in urban areas. As a dramatic example, after military operations ended in Sur, the historical centre of Diyarbakır in the Southeast region, the Ministry of Environment and Urban Affairs, relying on the Cabinet Decree no. 2016/869,[7] expropriated 6.300 parcels across the destroyed zones. Many residents therein were displaced and forced to move to other parts of the country. OHCHR (2018), relying on the UNOSAT analysis of successive imagery between November 2016 and June 2017, reports that 802 buildings in total were razed in Sur (para. 112).

Indirect Forfeiture by Trustees: In commercial literature, a trustee is a person or entity that holds the legal title to a trust property. It is rather seen as something relating to bankruptcy. Erdoğan regime, however, made the term trustee very popu-

---

5. Law no. 6721 was published in the Official Gazette of 28 June 2016, with no.29 756.
6. Cabinet Decree no.2018/11 995 was published in the Official Gazette of 24 June 2018, with no. 30 458.
7. Cabinet Decree no. 2016/869 was published in the Official Gazette of 25 March 2016, with no. 29 664.

lar in its "economic terrorism" against dissents through mass forfeiture and seizures.

Although it was introduced on 1 June 2005 within the article 133 of the Turkish Code of Penal Procedure (TCPP),[8] "appointing a trustee for the administration of a firm" as a preventive measure was revived by the Erdoğan regime. In principle, in case of strong suspicion of terrorist activities of any private company, the article allows to place it in government conservatorship through appointed trustees.

Available evidence indicates that the government implemented the huge part of the forfeiture programme through distortion of the original purpose of trustee procedure within the TCPP. From their viewpoint, it was a necessary (!) to give forfeitures at least a veneer of legality. It is also true that recent forfeiture operations have seriously distorted the focus and priorities of law enforcement in Turkey.

Moreover, by 2015, "Penal Judges of Peace" (not courts, but individual judges embedded within the ruling party)[9] with reference to article 133 of the TCPP, began appointing trustees to the companies including media outlets based on the suspicion of a linkage with the Gülen Movement. Such a "suspicion" is even interpreted by these judges as a convincing proof of being a member of a terrorist organisation.

By the way, let us remember that, in a criminal proceeding, in the sense of "burden of proof", the prosecutor must prove that someone is guilty beyond a reasonable doubt. But under TCPP, the court can take someone's cash, car or home merely by showing that it is more likely than not that the property was

---

8. The Law (TCPP) was published in the Official Gazette of 17 December 2004, with no. 25 673.
9. *Sulh Ceza Hakimi* in Turkish.

connected to a crime. Contrary to this, you have to prove your innocence, if you are lucky enough.

In the case of *Koza İpek*, the elderly family members were not lucky enough: the trustee seized the family home because it belonged to the legal entity of the company, and as a result the family members were not allowed to enter their own house for a while, even though they were never charged with or convicted of any wrongdoing at that time. *(See figure 6, page 222)*

GENERAL TRUSTEE: SAVINGS DEPOSIT INSURANCE FUND

As the numbers of companies with a trustee increase, the government deemed to gather these companies under the overall ownership of the "Savings Deposit Insurance Fund" (TMSF), an institution which is highly incompetent in the field, for the sake of coordination of the forfeiture programme by one hand.

By the article 19 of the Decree Law no. 674 (adopted by Law no. 6758), the TMSF was designated as a "General Trustee", with a particular purpose of sales or liquidation, to head these companies that have been managed by individual trustees. This will also be the norm for all future trustee appointments during the SoE. Namely, in the context of the persecution of the Gülen Movement's followers, TMSF remains the sole responsible trustee to be appointed by the judges/courts throughout this period.

According to the 2nd Quarterly Report (April-June 2018)[10] issued by the TMSF, of 6 August 2018, a total of **1.207** corporate or individual enterprises from 44 provinces of Turkey were partially or fully transferred to the TMSF. TMSF fully took over 940 of these companies with the following financial summary (Table 2):

---

10. https://tmsf.org.tr/tr/Rapor/UcAylikRapor (Accessed: 31 October 2018).

Table 2: Overall Financial Profile of the Companies Forfeited

Total asset size (appr.)	52.8 billion TL
Total equity (appr.)	20.6 billion TL
Total turnover (appr.)	14.6 billion TL
Total number of emplpyees	46.465

Data Source: 2nd Quarterly Report by the TMSF Turkey (2018)

Thus, during those two years of the SoE alone, the Erdoğan regime yielded about 53 billion TL ($10 billion at that time) worth of forfeited wealth or property. That amount is five times bigger than the annual revenue of the Motor Vehicles Tax in 2017, 10.8 billion TL.[11] The figures will be even higher when the value of the assets (schools, dormitories, universities, hospitals etc.) that were put under the disposal of the National Estate is included. An updated list of companies can be found on the TMSF website.[12]

The figures in Table 2 do not include those of the "Bank Asya" as its story of being forfeited began in 2014: Bank Asya was an interest-free "participation bank" operating with a capital (paid-in) of 900 million TL, 54.75 % of its shares being publicly held. In the days following the grand corruption scandals of December 2013, then-Prime Minister Erdoğan accused the Gülen Movement of organising a conspiracy against the government while targeting Bank Asya relentlessly for its alleged ties to this movement. Public institutions then started to withdraw their deposits from Bank Asya, the bank's standard agreement with the Ministry of Finance for some regular operation was cancelled, in the Stock Exchange of İstanbul (BIST), public trad-

---

11. Annual Activity Report-2017 by the Turkish Revenue Administration: https://www.gib.gov.tr (Accessed: 25 October 2018).
12. https://www.tmsf.org.tr/tr/Sirket/Kayyim (Accessed: 22 June 2018).

ing in Bank Asya was suspended three times and businessmen were pushed to withdraw their money from the bank.

Furthermore, the BDDK handed over the control of Bank Asya to the TMSF on 29 May 2015. Subsequently, BDDK terminated the bank's license to banking operations on 22 July 2016. Bank Asya was shut down by Decree Law no. 667 of 23 July 2016 and those depositing money in Bank Asya after December 2013 have started to be prosecuted with the allegation of being linked to the "Fethullahist Terror Organisation". Finally, the Commerce Court No. 1 of İstanbul resolved on the bankruptcy of Bank Asya on 16 December 2017.

When it was taken over by the TMSF, Bank Asya was operating with an asset value of 10.7 billion TL (appr. $4 billion at that time) and 3.067 personnel in their HQ and 200 branches.[13]

Turning to the subject matter, when the sales and transfers are accomplished, historians may wish to record this case as the most sizable capital shift from the corporate management to the agents of the DUP activities in which non-producers achieve an asymmetric, exploitative economic position vis-à-vis producers. But this is a topic for another study that economists may conduct in the future.

Decree Law no. 675 further expanded the trustee appointing procedure to the companies shared by the natural or legal persons affiliated with the Gülen Movement with a rate less than fifty percent. According to article 9(1) of the Decree, "with the aim of management and representation of these shares," the TMSF shall be appointed by the court or judge as a trustee in accordance with the article 133 of the TCPP.

As for the patents, trademarks and designs, on 21 of July

---

13. The latest Consolidated Activity Report (April-June 2015) of Bank Asya can be seen from: https://www.kap.org.tr/tr/Bildirim/493376 (Accessed: 15 11. 2018).

2017, Minister of Science, Industry and Technology announced that the legal rights over 734 trademarks, 72 designs (intellectual property), and 15 patents associated with the Gülen Movement were handed over by the Turkish Patent and Trademark Institution to the TMSF. 1.687 trademarks and 29 designs were transferred to the Treasury as well.[14] Nevertheless, it has remained uncertain how this transfer was achieved due to the lack of any authorization to do so.

Although it was originally in charge of "protecting the rights of depositors" and assigned "to contribute to confidence and the stability of the banking system" in Turkey, the TMSF has since become some kind of "CEO" of private companies ranging from simple restaurants to big companies of the country like *Boydak* (furniture), *Koza İpek* (media, gold mining, energy), *Dumankaya* (housing, construction), *Kaynak* (publication, stationery), etc. Not only the legal framework, but also public institutions were distorted from their original purposes.

Of course, the patronage of the TMSF is not intended as a permanent status. Forfeited property providing a new source of business should have been transferred as soon as possible to the loyal AKP supporters. To this end, article 81 of the Decree Law no. 680 dated 6 January 2017, with the exception of the ones subjected to direct forfeiture, allows the release or liquidation of these companies based on the approval of the Minister affiliated to the TMSF.[15]

The call for the companies or assets that are deemed ready for sale are published on the website of the TMSF. However, in the sense of transparency, crucial points are alarming: the

---

14. http://www.hurriyet.com.tr/bakan-acikladi-fetoye-ait-734-marka-72-tasarim-ve-15-patent-tmsfye-devredildi-40 526 923 (Accessed: 20 8. 2017).
15. With the Presidential Decree no. 2018/1, the TMSF was "linked" to the President on 15 July 2018.

procedures governing the sales, award criteria, total income generated by the sales and the identity of successful tenderers. Because of the strategic goals of the forfeiture programme, as explained above, no award notice has been published.

On the other hand, recent developments following the elections of 24 June won by Erdoğan showed that the TMSF is going to continue to operate as the General Trustee under the Palatial regime: the provisional article 1(1) of Law no. 7145,[16] taking the legacy of the crackdown forward to the post-SoE allows the procedure to be applied for a "three-year period" as from the publication date of the law, 31 July 2018. This implies the forfeiture programme has not ended yet.

CONCLUSION: TRANSITION FROM THE HOUSE OF PRAYERS TO THE "DEN OF ROBBERS"

Thus, as it is the case at the top of the state, through forfeiture of dissidents' properties, supporters ultimately turn into noble robbers. Hereafter, they are expected to vest their interests in the AKP remaining in office, even in case an electoral defeat occurred. It is not of much importance that mass forfeitures may create a regime of commercial uncertainty and confusion in the eye of foreign investors.

Here is the ultimate destination of a hegemonic Islamist party of which agents mostly have a religious background that aggrandises praying for forgiveness, afterlife preparedness, and altruistic behaviours. In fact, no surprise in their arrival to that point, at least for those who heard what Jesus Christ said to people of the Temple.

When we connected the dots, it would easily be seen that all

---

16. Law no. 7145 was published in the Official Gazette of 31 July 2018, with no. 30 495.

the operations in the context of the asset forfeiture were parts of a much bigger programme in order to make the country safe for Erdoğan's Palatial capitalism. In such a DUP mode of economy, stealing is marginally more valuable than regular economic activity.

CHAPTER FIVE

The commonwealth of Erdoğan: Milking public enterprises through Turkey wealth fund*

---

* Initial version of this chapter first appeared as an article at the PPJ website on 29.9.2017.

> *The life of the bandit is the life of the werewolf, who is precisely neither man nor beast, and who dwells paradoxically within both while belonging to neither.*
>
> Giorgio Agamben

SOVEREIGN WEALTH FUNDS

*T*HE FUNDS DIVERTED FROM 1MDB WERE USED FOR *the personal benefit of the co-conspirators and their relatives and associates, including to purchase luxury real estate in the United States and overseas, pay gambling expenses at Las Vegas casinos, acquire more than $200 million in artwork, purchase lavish gifts for family members and associates, [...] 1MDB maintained no interest in these assets and saw no returns on these investments..."*

The above findings are quoted from the Plaintiff[1] brought by the U. S. attorney to the court to forfeit assets involved in and traceable to an international conspiracy to launder money misappropriated from "1MDB" which is now the focus of money-laundering probes in at least six countries.

1MDB here stands for "1Malaysia Development Berhad", a

---

1. https://www.justice.gov/opa/press-release/file/973 671/download (Accessed: 20 9. 2017).

Sovereign Wealth Fund (SWF) wholly-owned by the government of Malaysia. From the file, we also learn the original mission of 1MDB: *"to pursue investment and development projects for the economic benefit of Malaysia and its people."* This case may give an insight into how SWFs with low transparency and accountability could serve to fuel astonishing greed of rulers and their relatives.

SWFs, especially from the start of the 21st century, have come to be seen as an important investment tool to ensure a better utilisation of economic surpluses of countries. Employing these surpluses strategically, allows a SWF to invest in a broad spectrum of assets including airports, energy, finance, real estate, equity markets, and so forth. SWF assets – and the returns they generate- can have a significant effect on public finances, monetary conditions, external accounts and balance sheet linkages with the rest of the world (IMF, 2013).

According to a special report[2] by *Preqin*, a private data provider currently tracking 76 active SWFs, their total assets reached $6.59 trillion in March 2017.

The International Working Group of Sovereign Wealth Funds (IWG) [International Forum of SWFs (IFSWF) since 2009] defines SWFs as *"special purpose investment funds or arrangements that are owned by the general government. Created by the general government for macroeconomic purposes, SWFs hold, manage, or administer assets to achieve financial objectives, and employ a set of investment strategies that include investing in foreign financial assets."*

In literal terms, SWFs are large pools of savings that can be used for a variety of investment purposes, both within and outside the owning state (Backer, 2015). Regardless of the gov-

---

2. http://docs.preqin.com/reports/Preqin-Special-Report-Sovereign-Wealth-Funds-August-2017.pdf (Accessed: 20 9.2017).

ernance framework, a particular "saving" must be available to establish such an entity.

SWFS are diverse in their origins, objectives, and investment strategies. They generally take the form of state-owned corporations with distinct legal persona. The term "sovereign" refers to the fact that the asset owner is not a private corporation, but a sovereign government. SWFS typically gather one or more of the following national assets from which the saving comes:

1. *revenues extracted from a particular natural source such as oil and gas,*

2. *excess foreign exchange reserves and budget contributions.*

As for the main objectives of SWFS, IMF (2013) identifies five categories: (1) stabilization fund, (2) savings fund, (3) development fund, (4) pension reserve fund, and (5) reserve investment company. These objectives, however, can be best achieved in practice by directly associating them with governance structure, investment strategy, and transparency requirements.

Despite the rhetorical flourishes and good intentions with which it was created, SWFS have not produced much wealth to the people of the owner states. Today, the leading concern to which SWFS give rise is mismanagement of investments and corruption including money laundering, bogus transactions, and funding lavish lifestyles of a small group at the top. This is especially the case for the SWFS established in developing countries where the biggest weaknesses are with respect to accountability and associated transparency.

Against the boom of SWF affairs with corrupted forms, the U. S. Department of Justice (DoJ) announced in 2008 that investigations into passive and active investments involving SWFS were "at the top of the Justice Department's hit list" (Cornelius, 2008).

Consequently, in an IMF-sponsored conference in Santiago, Chile, IWG introduced a voluntary set of "Generally Accepted Principles and Practices" (GAPP) concerning the governance, accountability and investment operations of SWFS. Thus, the rules of game surrounding their activities have been codified within the **Santiago Principles** of October 2008.[3]

Although Santiago Principles have a "voluntary" character and are not internationally binding, a higher compliance with its GAPPs is recognised a prerequisite for entry into U. S. and European markets. To this end, C. Linaburg and M. Maduell developed an index which is known as the "Linaburg-Maduell Transparency Index" (LMTI), under the sponsorship and publishing of the SWF Institute (SWFI).[4]

The LMTI rates transparency based on the analysis of satisfaction of 10 fundamental principles by the SWFS. The scoring of each point of the index results in one point and the ranking goes from 0 to 10. SWFI recommends that a SWF must have a minimum value of "8" to be considered adequately transparent. The LMTI therefore serves as a standard global benchmarking tool. The SWFI publishes the LMTI ratings on its website on a quarterly basis.

Since 2008 therefore, both the U. S. DoJ and SEC (Securities and Exchange Commission) have intensified their spotlights over the SWFS' activities for possible violations of the "Foreign Corrupt Practices Act". It is crucial when SWF employees use the American financial system for corruption as "The Foreign

---

3. http://www.ifswf.org/sites/default/files/santiagoprinciples_0_0.pdf (Accessed: 20 9. 2017).
4. LMTI: https://www.swfinstitute.org/statistics-research/linaburg-maduell-transparency-index/(Accessed: 20 9. 2017).

Sovereign Immunities Act" does not grant any immunity to government officials working on behalf of a foreign state.

Of course, the above considerations do not necessarily imply that SWFS would not contribute to overall growth level and financial diversity in quest of source, but simply that they do not comprise an adequate response to increasing economic stress in a country with no "surplus" in economic sense. For a country, the amount of surplus produced is a crucial determinant of many other aspects of the economy and social system of a people.

A staple economy requires investment in "productive" activities rather than unviable vanity projects which are highly associated with "rent-seeking" activities as the case in Turkey. We therefore suggest, when intelligently used, SWFS may contribute positively to this end and macro-finance policies of governments.

But the opposite may also be true: SWFS may play a role in the transfer of national assets to the pocket of the ruler and his collaborators and thus turn into a predatory device. To see how such a thing occurs, we will analyse the conditions under which "Turkey Wealth Fund" was established and legal framework under which it operates.

TURKEY WEALTH FUND (TWF)

When Law no. 6741 on the "Establishment of Turkey Wealth Fund Management Joint Stock Company" ("TWF" or "the Company" hereinafter)[5] was adopted by the parliament on 19 8. 2016, one month after the abortive coup of 15 July, it was hard not to notice that a significant amount of the governmental

---
5. Law no. 6741 was published in the Official Gazette of 26 8. 2016, with no. 29 813.

revenue would make its way into the hands of Erdoğan. Then, let us have a look how it may come true.

As is known, most SWFs have been established in countries that are rich in natural resources, with oil-related SWFs being the most common and largest group. These include the funds sponsored by the Arab Gulf countries, Russia and the ex-Soviet republics, Malaysia, Brunei, and Norway. A newer set of funds has recently been established in response to discoveries of major new resource endowments, particularly natural gas, but also oil, coal, diamonds, copper, and other minerals. A second important group of SWFs includes those financed out of accumulated foreign currency reserves resulting from persistent and large net exports, especially the funds based in Singapore, Korea, China, and other East-Asian exporters (Bortolotti et. al, 2014).

From this angle, a "third way" seems to be incompatible, at least with the generally accepted definition of the SWF. So, as seen from the following figure, SWFs rely on the reserves saved from either commodity (hydrocarbon or other) or non-commodity (foreign exchange) assets, nothing else.

However, as the 32nd member of the "International Forum of Sovereign Wealth Funds" (IFSWF), TWF represents the third way by source of capital. Such SWFs could then be labelled a "wealth fund without wealth" as they are emerging in countries with large deficits and deep debt (Milhench, 2017).

In lack of any surplus reserve or advantageous revenue resource, the TWF was founded with an enterprise capital of 50 million TL paid by the Privatization Fund. The source therefore comes from the key Turkish public assets which are among the largest in Turkey. And the Company, pursuant to article 1(1) of the Law, will manage those assets in order to;

1. *contribute to the diversity and depth of the capital market instruments,*

2. *bring the public assets of the country into the economy,*

3. *provide foreign resource, and*

4. *participate in strategic, large-scale investments.*

The latter was notably emphasised by the government spokesmen with reference to ongoing projects such as airports, seaports, roads, and railways most of which are undertaken by AKP-sided contractors, and unviable "vanity projects" like *Channel Istanbul*.

Article 4(1) of the Law assigns the TWF to keep the following revenue resources:

a. *the institutions and assets which fall within the scope and programme of privatization and decided by the High Board of Privatization to be transferred to the TWF and cash surplus decided by the High Board of Privatization to the TWF,*

b. *the surplus income, resources and assets which are in the possession of public entities and institutions within the public sectors and which are decided by the Cabinet to be transferred to the TWF or managed by the Company,*

c. *the funds and resources which are provided from national and international money and capital mar-*

kets by the TWF without seeking the permissions and approvals stated in the related legislations, and

d. the funds and resources provided through other resources in addition to the money and capital markets.

Subsequent to these provisions, as of today, we have a long list of the national companies which have been transferred massively to the TWF's property (Table 3).

Table 3: TWF-owned Companies with their Current Values

	Companies/Enterprises	Tresury Share Transferred (%)	Capital (paid-in) (million TL)	Asset Value (million TL)
1	Ziraat Bankası	100	5.100	434.275
2	Halkbank	51.11	1.250	305.350
3	BOTAS Pipeslines	100	4.145	30.292
4	Turkish Petroleum (TPAO)	100	3.000	10.982
5	Postal Services (PTT)	100	1.534	5.567
6	Istanbul Stock Exchange (BIST)	73.60	423	11.882
7	Turkish Airlines (THY)	49.12	1.380	68.467
8	Turkish Satellite (TURKSAT)	100	1.955	2.697
9	Turkish Telecom	6.68	3.500	26.874
10	Eti Mining	100	600	3.857
11	Turkish Tea (Çaykur)	100	1767	3.172
12	Turkish Maritime	49	?	?
13	Kayseri Sugar Factory	10	?	?
14	Izmir Port of Turkish Railways	?	?	?
	Total		24.654	903.415

Data Source: Official Gazette, TWF website, Companies' Annual Reports of 2017.
Note: Asset Value refers to sum total of the assets in the year-end balance sheets.

The first eleven rows of Table 3 show the list of the companies transferred by the Cabinet Decree no.2017/9756.[6] The last three in *italic*, however, were transferred by the High Board of Privatisation on 3 February 2017. Unusually, decisions concerning these transfers (decisions no. 2017/3 – 4-5) were pub-

---

6. Cabinet Decree no. 2017/9756 was published in the Official Gazette of 5 February 2017, with no. 29 970 (M).

lished neither in the Official Gazette nor on the website of the Privatisation Administration. These enterprises have not published any balance sheet indicating their capital and asset values.

Various immovable properties in 46 land plots belonging to the National Estates in Antalya, Aydın, Isparta, Istanbul, İzmir, Kayseri, and Muğla, amounting 2.292.815 m2 in total, were also transferred to the TWF by the Cabinet Decree no. 2017/9756.

Within the Cabinet Decree no. 2017/9758, a cash amount of 3 billion TL belonging to the "Defence Industry Support Fund" (DISF) was transferred to the TWF for a three-month usage.[7]

Decree Law no. 680 of 6 January 2017 transferred all the licenses of winning games operated by the National Lottery (article 82), and license for horse racing of the Turkey Jockey Club including relevant facilities for a duration of 49 years as from 1 January, 2018 (article 77) to the TWF.

The TWF has thus become a fund with about $6.3 billion of equity capital and approximately $200 billion of asset size by 2017, plus a large number of real estate and licenses generating high revenue with almost no cost. Those transfers to the TWF cannot be considered a simple transfer of the ownership or usage, but of "property" in the legal sense. Article 5(1) of the Law reads that all the assets and rights are to be registered by relevant authorities on behalf of the TWF's legal entity. Not revenue stream, but the whole company!

As we underlined above, SWFs are generally used by countries with large external surpluses generated from natural resources like oil or gas. TWF, however, is owned by the Turkish government operating no such surplus, but dealing with chronic budgetary deficits. Therefore, it is normal to see that the list above does not refer to any saving or surplus in an economic sense

---

7. Cabinet Decree no. 2017/9758 was published in the Official Gazette of 5 February 2017, with no. 29 970 (M).

and that the TWF's resources consist primarily of non-liquid assets. *(See figure 7, page 223)*

Thus, the TWF can be considered as the first in its kind as a fund grabbing state-owned real and financial assets in lack of any budgetary or commodity saving.

From an optimistic point of view, as the article 2(3)/a of the Law implies, some of the TWF assets can either be expected to be sold, to generate cash or to be used as collateral to secure much needed funding, especially for heavy-cost infrastructure projects. But, instead of the TWF, both could be achieved in practice by the Privatisation Fund and/or Treasury borrowing, more or less, in a fair, transparent, and auditable manner. There would be no need to deviate from the principle of the "Unity of Treasury" if the original intention was to utilise national assets as a rainy day fund for the short term.

Then, let us connect the dots: contrary to that of the Privatisation Fund, in release of public assets, what "safety" the TWF provides is exemption from the audit of Turkish Court of Accounts (TCA), a constitutional auditing body operating on behalf of the parliament, as well as competitive tendering procedures applied.

That is to say, since article 8(5) of Law no. 6741 immunes the TWF and the Company from the audit of TCA, procedures of Law no. 4046 on privatisation, if you deemed politically correct to make one of your guys owner of any public asset, to be on the safe side, you transfer it to the TWF and then the TWF, with no competition, no audit trail, even no due diligence, delivers it directly to this guy.

On the other hand, it is also not clear how the TWF will succeed in its objectives relying on these assets. As Dedeoğlu (2017) rightly highlights, it is uncertain how exactly large companies' and state-owned enterprises' shares would be used to create funding as the companies concerned, with the exception of Turkish Airlines, are not listed in the stock exchange. Their shares are not traded, and thus these companies do not have market prices. They are not subject to international audit or rating. Therefore, a proper securitisation seems to be impossible, at least in short term.

It is very obvious that a portfolio based on such shares does not attract foreign professional investors, but is likely to increase political control over the companies. Therefore, direct releases to domestic "entrepreneurs" in a discretionary manner seem to be the most possible way the government stays on. Such, however, is financially modernised form of the "predatory state" (see chapter 7).

In parallel to this, article 3(1)/ç of the TWF Internal Regulation *(İç Tüzük)* designates fund generation from "non-equity and out of financial market resources" pointing to the reliance on some doubtful transfers. Given these provisions, one can talk about money laundering or illegal cash transfer.

As it is demonstrated above, the TWF lacks main advantages of other SWFs and heavily relies on consuming the existing reserves (expenditure) instead of generating financial pay-offs and/or reserving incomes for future generations (saving). Expenditure through TWF mechanisms, however, ultimately results in the unaccountable disappearance of huge sums of national resource from state coffers.

Therefore, typical terms like "parallel budget" or "off-budget account" do not and cannot explain the nature of a SWF with such traits. However, in both Turkish media and academia, less attention has been devoted to understand this particular characteristics of the TWF, so many have focused on how the TWF may create a funding vehicle by leveraging up public assets or whether it is expected to take some budgetary and Central Bank functions.

Of course, public assets can be utilised as a funding vehicle provided operations are transparent, auditable, and involving officials remain accountable. We then should really focus on the governance framework and audit of the TWF operations with a focus to some core GAPPs of the Santiago Principles.

GOVERNANCE FRAMEWORK

Even as it begins to operate, TWF has also begun to be mired in accusations of corruption. The main reason was directly associated with how it is set up in governance terms. The tone adopted by Law no. 6741 making less reference to the reporting, accountability, and transparency requirements was also a cause for concern in this respect. The Cabinet Decree no. 2016/9429[8] concerning the organisational structure and operations of the Company, however, just refers to the financial reporting that has been neither audited nor publicised yet.

As referred above, SWFs are supposed to adhere to the Santiago Principles. We learn from the IFSWF that TWF also voluntarily agrees to uphold the GAPPs as a prerequisite for membership.

At first, GAPP-1 refers to a "sound legal framework" supporting SWF's operation and the achieving its stated objective(s). When the provisions of the Law is scrutinised, it is very hard to find a "soundness" concerning the relationship between the TWF and other state bodies Ministry of Treasury and Finance, Central Bank, Capital Market Authority, and İstanbul Stock

---

8. Cabinet Decree no.2016/9429 was published in the Official Gazette of 9 November 2016, with no.29 883.

Exchange of which the head occupies one seat in the TWF's board of directors.

In the latter, especially, as the Treasury's share of 73.6 % was already transferred to the TWF, it remains uncertain how potential conflict of interests/roles can be avoided. This picture is clearly incompatible with GAPP-1. So the ultimate objective of the SWFs can only be achieved if they are managed within a sound governance structure and with appropriate investment strategies (IMF, 2013).

As associated with the mentioned criteria, GAPP-**16** also requires public disclosure of the governance framework and objectives as well as the manner in which the SWF's management operates to be "operationally independent" from the owner, i. e. the government.

The TWF, despite its separate entity, was first structured under the Prime Ministry (PM) and is operated by the Company with a board of directors consisting of a minimum of five members, president and a general manager all of whom are appointed by the PM. Secondary legislation concerning the operational rules and procedures of the Company is decided by the Cabinet in the form of the "Government Decree" while the TWF's Internal Regulation is foreseen to be issued by the Company itself.

When it comes to the management of the assets held by the TWF and its sub-funds, article 3(2) of the Law requires "A 3-Year Strategic Investment Plan" to be the norm. This plan is prepared by the Company's board of directors and is put into force with the Cabinet approval. However, no indication is found therein about whether the plan would be a "budget-supporting" tool despite GAPP-**3** asking SWF activities to be closely coordinated with the domestic fiscal and monetary authorities, to ensure consistency with the overall macroeconomic policies.

As evidence for those concerns, amid discussions and rumours concerning the best possible direction of the Strategic Investment Plan, the founder of the TWF, Mehmet Bostan, was dismissed on 7 September 2017. Some news in press[9] revealed that it was a result of strategic disputes over the TWF between President Erdoğan and PM Yıldırım.

This case even demonstrated that the TWF itself could be a cause of conflict within the government when it comes to the role it would play in the economy. Because of such a conflict, TWF's strategic investment plan which was sent to the PM Office on 10 April 2017 has not been approved yet, and no progress has been made on the matter to this day [December 2018]. This might negatively affect the operability of the TWF and renders inactive until the time the dust settled.

Resolutions (!) came in sequence: first, thanks to the new Presidential System-with-no-PM, such possible disputes will automatically disappear in the future. By article 37(1) of the Presidential Decree no. 1,[10] the TWF became an affiliated body of the Palace. Of course, such can be seen as "normal" because the PM no longer exists and the TWF should then be assigned to a top level authority. But Erdoğan went three steps further going beyond this organisational necessity:

1. *Presidential Decree no. 3*[11] *concerning the appointment procedures for the high-rank officials reads that the chair and members of the TWF are to be assigned by the President.*

---

9. https://www.bloomberg.com/news/articles/2017-09-08/turkey-said-to-replace-wealth-fund-chief-amid-internal-strife (Accessed: 8 September 2017).
10. Presidential Decree no. 1 was published in the Official Gazette of 10 July 2018, with no. 30 474.
11. Presidential Decree no. 3 was published in the Official Gazette of 10 July 2018, with no. 30 474.

2. *Presidential Decision no. 2018/162,[12] amending article 13(2) of the Cabinet Decree no. 2016/9429, assigns Erdoğan himself (yes, himself!) as the chairperson of the executive board.*

3. *Presidential Decision no. 2018/163 of the same date assigns his son-in-law, Berat Albayrak (Minister of Treasury and Finance at the same time), as his deputy in the management of the TWF, while Trade Registry Gazette of 29 11. 2018 (no. 9713) announced full authorisation of the son-in-law in the management and representation of the TWF and its sub-funds.*

First, to the *Transparency International* (2009) defining the "Grand Corruption" as "acts committed at a high level of government that distort policies or the functioning of the state, enabling leaders to benefit at the expense of the public good," and

Second to the GAPP-22 asking the SWFs to "have a framework that identifies, assesses, and manages the risks of its operations." Recent changes in the managerial structure of the TWF imply that the "framework" concerned will be designed at the Palace as a "family business." Erdoğan and – likely- his advisory team must have thought that a TWF led by the President and his son-in-law gives assurance to the foreign investors.

Commentary of the GAPP-22, however, draws attention to the reputational risks as one of the main dangers that SWFs face in their operations: "Reputational risk is the potential that negative publicity regarding SWF's business practices,

---

12. Presidential Decisions no. 2018/162 – 163 were published in the Official Gazette of 12 9. 2018, with no. 30 533, while the changes in the management structure was registered by the Trade Registry Gazette dated 20 9. 2018, with no. 9664.

whether true or untrue, may cause a decline in investment returns, costly litigation, or a loss of counterparties, or impair the home country government's international standing." No need for further comment.

As can be seen, this organisational framework adopted by Law no. 6741, when combined with the recent changes by the Palace, does not leave any room to consider the TWF having a substantial, or at least operational, autonomy from the Erdoğan family, nor is its funds well protected from use by them as it needs them for short term projects or to make up monetary shortfalls.

Regardless of the governance framework, the operational management of an SWF should be conducted on an "independent" basis to minimize potential political influence or interference that could hinder the achievement of the SWF's objectives (IMF, 2013).

OPERATIONS AND INVESTMENTS

With regards to the operations of the TWF and its sub-funds, the TWF published an internal regulation in the Turkish Trade Registry on 30 1. 2017. This was followed by the TWF decision of 10 April 2017 concerning the establishment of various sub-funds:

1. *Market Stability and Equilibrium*

2. SME *Financing*

3. *License and Concessions*

4. Mining, and according to the Trade Registry of 29 March 2018 with no. 9547

5. Istanbul Stock Exchange (BIST) Venture Capital Investment Fund

With the exception of "Market Stability and Equilibrium", other sub-funds are foreseen to be operated under the title of "Market Depth and Equilibrium." It is unknown what the added value of this differentiation was.

Regulations governing the sub-funds were also published in the Turkish Trade Registry dated 1 June 2017. It is understood from the regulations with similar content that, despite different titles, all sub-funds seem to be tasked with some speculative operations in stock markets.

To this end, according to article 4 of the TWF's Internal Regulation, "participation shares" will be issued on the basis of the revenues, sources and assets of the TWF. These certificates comprising the portfolio of the sub-funds are foreseen to be invested in the assets and transactions listed in their regulation, for example, money and capital markets instruments, public borrowing instruments, gold and precious mines, and so forth.

As discussed above, this base represents the darkest side of the operations assigned to sub-funds. So it is well known that, in lack of any proper market price, independent audit, and rating for the TWF assets most of which are state-owned enterprises not listed in the stock exchange, associated "shares" are incapable of attracting professional investors.

Moreover, neither the TWF nor government spokesmen have disclosed any information to the public on the progress that had been achieved so far. Let us clarify: who are the entrepreneurs invested in the shares concerned? What about the size and value of the shares sold so far? What is the last updated portfolio of the sub-funds? Were 3 billion TL paid back to the DISF when the three-month period expired and what is the return?

Such questions do not accommodate any accusation but fall under the GAPP-17: "Relevant financial information regarding the SWF should be publicly disclosed to demonstrate its economic and financial orientation, so as to contribute to the stability of international financial markets and enhance trust of recipient countries."

Of course, real estates and game licenses can easily be priced comparing to the companies, but this remains instrumental only for selling these assets to investors without any further income stream. Moreover, article 11(j) of the Internal Regulation accepts the expenditures like commission or brokerage fees as eligible if they are paid for "selling/buying and leasing transactions concerning real estate investments." Such is also the norm for the sub-funds' operations.

How should the signals given by these regulations be interpreted under these circumstances? The following may be the answer that suits best to the corrupted conditions under which the Erdoğan regime survives: This is clearly an open invitation to the "entrepreneurs" seeking opportunities of money laundering, or alternatively, these bogus shares will be used to import some cash amount of the Erdoğan family and its associates into Turkey. You then remember article 3(1)/ç of the TWF Internal Regulation allowing "transfer of funds out of money and equity markets."

Let us look at the critical question: how would the TWF make the nation wealthier, as a wealth fund seeded with public assets? Interestingly, neither the TWF Internal Regulation nor regulations of the sub-funds do indicate how possible returns from those "investments" to be associated with the major objectives of the TWF listed in article 1(1) of Law no. 6741.

Of course, this association could be realised in practice through a three-year Strategic Investment Plan, but as discussed above, it seems highly ambiguous. Furthermore, uniform articles (3.8) in the regulations of the sub-funds imply that the Board of Directors may assign specific strategic targets for them while the list of eligible expenditures, even implicitly, does not refer to the provision of finance for infrastructure, energy, technology, telecommunication sectors, or any contribution to the general budget in this respect.

However, uniform articles, for example 11(1)/t of the TWF Internal Regulation, allow the TWF and its sub-funds to pay *"other expenditures to which the consent is given by the Board of Directors."*

Relying on this discretionary wideness, officials heading the TWF and its sub-funds, without fear of being prosecuted at least in Turkey, may involve, for example, the purchase of luxury real estate, paying gambling expenses, buying some artwork, the purchase of lavish gifts for family members and associates etc. In case any audit mission, there is no alarm since the auditors can only be able to check whether a written consent of the Board of Directors is found in the file.

Concluding again, TWF and its sub-funds lack any visible mechanism channelling their returns to the wealth of the nation.

AUDITING ON BEHALF OF THE PARLIAMENT

The TWF and its sub-funds are exempted from the audit of the TCA. The Significance of this audit comes from the fact that the TCA as the Auditor General, carries out its audit missions "on behalf of the parliament." That comprises one of the most crucial parts of the "budget right" and Turkish Constitution authorises the TCA only to do so.

In accordance with this perspective, as well as the conventional state organisations such as Treasury, Ministry of Finance, and Central Bank, paragraph (a) of article 4(1) of the TCA reads that *"[...] joint-stock companies established by special laws and of its capital directly or indirectly owned by the public sector [...]"* are subject to the audit of the TCA.[13]

Furthermore, the sub-paragraph [annexed by article 19 of Law no. 6661] of the (ç) says *"the companies along with their subsidiaries and associates which have less than 50 % of the direct or indirect public share"* are subject to a kind of indirect audit based on the independent audit reports to be submitted to TCA. TCA thus reports its relevant findings to the parliament.

Whether SWF or any other, in the organisational structure of an entity spending public money, governing and "supervisory" functions should be segregated. The governing bodies constitute a system of delegated asset management responsibilities whereas the role of the supervisory body is to verify that the supervised unit is operating in accordance with the applicable laws and regulations (IMF, 2013). Supervisory bodies typically include:

1. *The "auditor general" is, in most countries, designated by the constitution and operates "on behalf of the parliament" or of the crown to audit the activities of the government including those of SWF, and ensures reporting of relevant findings to the parliament. That is the TCA*

---

13. Law no. 6085 (TCA) was published in the Official Gazette of 19 December 2010, with no. 27 790.

> *in Turkey which is however excluded from the audit of the TWF.*

2. *The "external auditor" is usually selected by the governing body representing the SWF, Company in Turkey. The external auditor audits the accounts of the SWF and its sub-funds "on behalf of the governing body" and verifies that it is managed within the rules and regulations set by the governing body. The external auditor therefore submits its audit report to the governing body. For TWF, that is the certified audit firm in charge of "independent audit" described in article 6(1) of Law no. 6741. Independent audit findings are necessarily addressed to the Board of Directors and ultimately to the investors in the market.*

3. *The "internal auditor" is appointed by the executive board and reports to it. The internal auditor supports the board in supervising the management of the SWF and verifying that internal regulations are adhered to. For the TWF, that is the internal audit function described in article 2(4) of Law no. 6741. Internal audit findings are necessarily addressed to the Board of Directors and/or the Audit Committee.*

In addition to those audit functions, article 6(2) of the law requires the financial statements and activities of the TWF, sub-funds, Company, and affiliated companies which are previously audited by the independent auditor to be "audited" again by at least three central auditors appointed by the PM (the Palace of today).

These auditors are required to be specialists in capital markets, finance, economy, banking, and development and to be "independent" in that mission. By the end of June of each year, they shall submit their reports to the Palace. Their findings are necessarily addressed to the owner of the TWF, i. e. the President, instead of the government which no longer exists.

The control mechanism, rather than "compliance audit", looks like a kind of "expert review" to be conducted by a civil servants team on behalf of the Palace holding their living wage in its hands. Nevertheless, overlapping audit missions do not necessarily maintain a quality assurance, but generally waste time, energy and money.

As is known, neither an independent audit nor an expert review is carried out on behalf of the Parliament. However, pursuant to the article 6(3) of the Law, both independent audit reports and expert reviews are sent by the PM (it is Palace today) to the Planning and Budget Commission of the Parliament so as to provide an "assurance" over the TWF operations by examining these reports.

The government (or the regime), as the legal owner of the TWF, is accountable to the Legislature and to the public for the TWF's declared objectives. But audit missions ensuring accountability are fulfilled under the patronage of the Palace. It is obvious that this leaves little way to verify how the public money is spent and violates the GAPP-10 on the "accountability".

On the other hand, article 11(1)/s of the TWF Internal Regulation reads that the independent auditor is paid by the Company. That is a normal procedure indeed, but the same article is found within the regulations of all the sub-funds. This overlapping implies that each sub-fund will be audited separately or that total audit cost are shared by the sub-funds. This may complicate the audit process.

For the financial year of 2016, we learned from the Turkey Trade Registry Gazette of 16 October 2017, that the Company, on behalf of the TWF, assigned an independent audit company, *Akis Bağımsız Denetim ve SMMM A. Ş.*, today's KPMG-Turkey, to perform the audit activity in question. However, no audit report was sent to the parliament for this year. As for the year 2017, the Trade Registry of 11 1. 2018 announces that *Güreli YMM ve Bağımsız Denetim Hizmetleri A. Ş.* was tasked with the annual audit mission while recent media news revealed that its report was sent to the parliament within a "confidential" file in October 2018. This indicates that the MPs will negotiate the report in a closed session and thus no information will be disclosed to the public.[14]

As can be seen, in the sense of auditing and reporting to the legislature, TWF clearly deviates from other SWFs in the world. This mechanism produces less evidence for those who want to be assured that TWF is doing right things and contradicts with the GAPP-6: "the governance framework for the SWF should be sound and establish a clear and effective division of roles and responsibilities in order to facilitate accountability and operational independence in the management of the SWF to pursue its objectives."

CONCLUSION: THEFT IS PROPERTY!

When he analysed the inequalities in ownership, Pierre-Joseph Proudhon, a French thinker of the 19th century, provocatively concludes that "property is theft!" But the Erdoğan regime in Turkey made the "theft" property. This is a trend that is going to continue and the TWF represents the last instance of the Erdoğanist hoax.

---

14. See, for example: https://www.demokrathaber.org/guncel/turkiye-varlik-fonu-yla-il-gili-denetim-raporu-gizli-h108 684.html (Accessed: 2 December 2018).

For a SWF organisation bearing numerous deviations from the core GAPPs of the Santiago Principles, it seems less possible to be considered adequately "transparent" to invest in European and US markets. Therefore, the TWF, as a fund owned by Turkey with an annual external financing deficit of around $30 billion, is expected to attract black money from the supposed "entrepreneurs" of the Middle East and Asia regions to plug the gap under a veneer of legality.

In addition to the lack of transparency and corporate governance practices, systemic uncertainties in securitisation of the assets under management leave less room for the TWF to play in the premier league of the SWFs. Although it voluntarily agrees to uphold the GAPPs, non-compliance with the international standards leads the TWF to operate as an "inward-focused" fund exposed to a wide range of risks such as legality, governance, corruption, etc.

However, all these likely explain why Erdoğan and his *mujahidin* sought such a funding vehicle under the SWF title. As such, the TWF is a product of the decay of the Turkish political economy and governance frameworks and provides adequate evidence of Erdoğan's continued commitment to the predation of the public assets. For those who opened their eyes to see, every aspect of Erdoğan's predatory tendencies is visible in the design of the TWF. As a naive muckraker, what we try to do here is to disclose some aspect of it.

CHAPTER SIX

The rise of "predatory government" in Turkey: An insight into the social background*

---

* The initial version of this chapter first appeared as an article on the PPJ website on 9.2.2018.

The predators are praying you don't educate your child.
Kwasie Kwaku

NATURE VS. NURTURE

For an arboreal primate, distance from trees is associated with mortal danger from terrestrial enemies. A being sleeping on the ground with no cover is more vulnerable to predation. That seems to be the norm of the natural selection in a wild habitat.

When it comes to public or private goods, this principle of natural selection does not work as they are unable to escape or hide themselves. It is only by moral conventions and/or some legal measures that predation can be prevented. Therefore, it is the "civil society", as an organised form of human gathering, to develop effective ways to minimize their common goods' risk of predation by greedy rulers at the top.

However, if all predation attempts are successful at a significant moment in space and time, this should raise questions on whether the evolved ways possess anti-predator traits as well as the quality of rulers and managers in positions of trust. In this sense, especially the last decade of Turkey under the authority of Erdoğan should be analysed from this point of view as a modern case study of leaders' appetite for predation.

PREDATION IN HUMAN GATHERINGS

Predation, in its initial usage, refers to violence-loaded activities like hunting, plundering, fighting, war-making and frames the relationship between the prey and predator, of course from the latter's angle. The term "predatory" therefore invokes a metaphor of predator and prey.

When we translate this into political science, predation refers to activities performed by those who control the state apparatus to plunder with less regard for the welfare of the citizenry than a predator has for the welfare of its prey. So the preoccupation of the ruling elite with rent seeking turns the rest of society into prey (Evans, 1989).

From this point of view, when any state extracted huge amounts of otherwise investable surplus and provided so little in the way of "collective goods" in return, it is called "predatory." In literature, Zaire under Mobutu (1965 – 1997), where predation was built from the absence rather than the presence of strong opposition, is considered an archetypal sample of the predatory state.

PREDATORY STATE

J. M. Shumba (2016), learning the lessons from Zimbabwe of Robert Mugabe,[1] identifies the predatory state as characterised by (1) party and military dominance in the state; (2)

---

1. Robert Mugabe (1924–), finally succumbing to the pressure of a military takeover and the humiliation of impeachment, resigned on 21 11. 2017, after 37 years of autocratic rule.

state-business relations shaped by domination and capture; and (3) state-society relations shaped by violence and patronage. The power elite, in alliance with local and international criminal syndicates, extracts high levels of rents from the state and economy and, in so doing, undermines the country's development potential.

Although the power is concentrated in the person of the ruler, he is not alone in predation because predatory regimes are run by predatory coalitions endorsing a "winner-takes-all" game of power. In such a regime, predation represents redistribution of income in favour of this coalition to the detriment of the majority of the population.

Rulers are predatory in that they always try to set terms of trade that maximise their personal gains, which, as Levi (1988) argues, require them to maximise state revenues. They do not always plunder, pillage, and exploit. However, each will "attempt to act like a discriminating monopolist, separating each group of constituents and devising property rights for each so as to maximise state revenue."

In Levi's viewpoint, rulers are chief executives of the polity. This sounds fine for rulers like Erdoğan of Turkey who said on 15 March 2015: "The Republic of Turkey should be governed like a company!"[2]

Nevertheless, budgets mean little for a predatory ruler, both in terms of fiscal discipline and of best possible allocation of resources. Rather, the main instinct governing the ruler can be summarised as "milking the state enterprises": drawing resources from the economic to the political sphere (Lundahl, 1997).

---

2. https://tr.sputniknews.com/turkiye/201503151 014 435 942/(Accessed: 5 February 2018). This word has almost come true after the election of 24 June 2018 giving way to gather all the Executive functions at the Palace.

Predatory rulers are also normal of "kleptocratic" regimes in which corruption flows from the top downwards because a kleprocrat ruler will usually not be able to prevent his underlings from following his example. All he can do is, as Lundahl (1997) suggests, to attempt to create some method in the madness as Mobutu said to Zairian civil servants: "if you want to steal, steal a little cleverly, in a nice way."

A predatory ruler needs to feather the nests of a fairly narrow coalition of supporters when he first comes to power. This leads to the control of markets, natural resources, public procurements, concessions, etc. The ruler thus ensures steady revenue streams through the monopoly of economic activity, and thereby longevity in the office. Widespread dissatisfaction and grievances in society, however, rarely lead to conflicts since the ruler controls the military and other apparatuses of repression, and "patronage" politics where community leaders and ethnic elites are bought off to ensure stability (de Soysa, 2017).

In a nutshell, the term predatory state (or government) refers to a condition in which corruption, inefficiency, and abuse of power mark political institutions. A predatory state typically lacks transparency and a system of checks and balances. It thus constricts markets because of arbitrariness and scares off both native and foreign investments due to a lack of equal treatment by the government.

POLITICAL-SOCIOLOGICAL DIMENSION

The predatory ruler operates in a particularly brutal and often destructive way in order to secure and maintain his wealth and lifetime in the office. Loyalty to the ruler is based neither on religion nor ideology, nor on having a unique personal mission or charismatic qualities, but instead on a mixture of fear and rewards. What distinguishes a predatory state is not only a failure to deliver developmental outcomes; "it is [that it] also kills, maims and terrorises its citizens" (Bratton & Masunungure, 2011).

At its worst, predatory rulers such as Erdoğan of Turkey systematically exclude, repress and kill their own citizens; often feeding political insecurity and leading to ruthless suppression of dissents. Being fair; his counterparts like Saddam in Iraq, Assad in Syria, and some more anti-western regimes in the Middle East and Africa deserve to be mentioned in this respect.

On the other hand, constant predation and/or confiscation of public/private goods allowed a "socio-economic homogeneity" among relatives, friends, and other allies of the ruling elite and gave them a sense of *community*. The predatory ruler maintains his power by catering to their demands. Hence, they gradually turn to people of the kind that have common interests.

FINANCIAL-ECONOMIC DIMENSION

In a predatory state, governmental authority faces few constraints and the exploitation of public and private resources for the gain of elite interests is embedded in institutionalised practices with greater continuity of individual leaders. In this regard, a predatory regime can be seen as the extreme opposite of "accountable" and/or "developmental" forms of government.

Predatory relationships between the state and individuals depend on the power of the state to grab or to appropriate coercively and the ability of the subject to resist or escape (Vahabi, 2016). Therefore, predatory ruler directs his attention to high-revenue public enterprises that can be controlled more or less easy. Such is traditionally realized through siphoning off the funds from them. Thus, as suggested above, resources are directed from the economic to the political sphere leaving little financial and human capital to flow into productive sectors.

As a result of this policy, the country's wealth continues to be concentrated in the hands of a small elite whose members use government positions for massive personal enrichment, and corruption continues to be common practice at all levels. Thus, the following message is given to the business world: huge amounts of money cannot be made by fair competition in the markets, but only through client affiliations with a political leader or party.

ERDOĞANIST PREDATION METHODS

As for the creation of methods that aim to serve to facilitate predation, there simply seems to be no end to human imagination. The list by Lundahl (1997) provides the most widely employed devices in an unexhausted manner: taxation, tax farming, smuggling, sales of public offices, confiscation, inflation as a tax, foreign and domestic loans, embezzlement of aid, unbudgeted funds, government contracts, milking state enterprises or government-owned corporations, etc.

Apart from the previous attempts, taking the advantages of the SoE, since the failed coup of 15 July, 2016, the Erdoğan regime has turned into the innovator of some new methods of predation such as

> 1. the "Asset Forfeiture Programme" to eradicate the economic capacity of dissents (Decree Law no. 667 of 22 July 2016) and the "trustee" appointment procedure that enables the government to have access to almost any pri-

vate property in the country in accordance with article 133 of the Code of Penal Procedures on the basis of the alleged linkage with terrorist organisations,

2. the TWF for siphoning off revenues from public enterprises (Law no. 6741, Cabinet Decree no. 2017/975; Cabinet Decree no. 2017/9758; and Decree Law no. 680), as examined in the previous chapter, the most representative device of Erdoğanist predation.

By the following provisions of Decree Law no. 696 dated 24 December 2017, remaining "gaps" seem to be plugged:

1. Despite particular protection of legislation and Islamic traditions (the foundation deed is treated as a godly document), forfeit of the assets of certain foundations (waqf, plural awqaf)[3] through transferring their shares represented by the General Directorate of Foundation at the board of Vakıfbank to the Treasury, and thus making their equity and legal entity controversial as returns of the shares concerned will go to the coffer of the state (article 6 amending Law no. 6219 on Vakıfbank),

2. Disregarding donors' will, transfer of donated monies – under the solidarity campaign for the martyrs and veterans of 15 July – in ad hoc bank accounts to the establishment of the "Solidarity Foundation for the Martyr Relatives and Veterans", a new pro-AKP player in the battle theatre to promote the so-called martyrs and veter-

---

3. Waqf: a dedication under which property is permanently allocated for charity or religious purposes. Properties in this category can only be utilised for the purposes to which they are dedicated.

ans of 15 July (article 128): 10 million TL will be used as the foundation asset legally while the balance is transferred after the completion of the legal establishment,[4]

3. Permission to the TWF and its affiliated companies to function as a central treasury in terms of debt management including debt transfer, lending foreign debt, and repayment guarantee (article 86 amending Law no.4749 on Public Finance and Debt Management), and

1. Disregarding the rights of shareholders, suppliers, customers, banks etc. , as well as the ISA-705 standard of IAASB (para. 8)[5] prohibition of auditor from expressing "Adverse Opinion" for the companies managed by the court-appointed government trustees in cases of fraud, false accounting, manipulation of share value, tax evasion, etc. (article 109 overruling the article 402(5) of Turkish Code of Commerce).

As mentioned in chapter 5, the TMV was established by Law no. 6721 on 28 June 2016 as a public foundation to be financed from the national budget and the staff be granted diplomatic immunity to facilitate abroad operations against the schools with alleged ties to the Gülen Movement. Therefore

---

4. In an interview with the AA on 27 1. 2017, then-Minister of Family and Social Policies said that, as of 20 1. 2017, it was 300.9 million Liras ($86 million at that time) deposited in bank accounts held by the Prime Ministry and the Ministry of Family and Social Policies and no part of this amount would be paid directly to the target group. https://www.aa.com.tr/tr/gunun-basliklari/malul-sayilmayan-terorle-mucadele-gazileri-icin-duzenleme-yaptik/735 895 %20 (Accessed: 31 October 2018)
5. ISA-705, para. 8 reads: "The auditor shall express an adverse opinion when the auditor, having obtained sufficient appropriate audit evidence, concludes that misstatements, individually or in the aggregate, are both material and pervasive to the financial statements."

2. *the transfer of 351 million* TL *(appr. $70 million at that time) from the Ministry of National Education to the* TMV's *bank account on 24 June 2018 (i. e. Election Day) by the Cabinet Decree no. 2018/11 995,*

can also be considered an indecent sample of predation of national resources – to forfeit abroad property of the Gülen-inspired schools.

Also note that, in this vein, the rhetoric of "war on terror" has remained as the government's stalking horse while the rule by decree laws under the SoE facilitates the process of grinding out private/public fortunes on predatory basis.

As the main methods were analysed in depth in the previous chapters concerning forfeiture and the TWF, we will rather try to get an insight into the social-cultural ground above which the electoral victories of the Erdoğan regime rise.

TOWARD A PREDATORY REGIME IN TURKEY

The predatory state as characterised by weak bureaucratic capacity and poor institutionalisation, allows the ruler unconstrained access to and to abuse national resources. Since the emergence of the central state organisations, predatory rulers often try to cheat individuals who are ultimately bearing the cost of the distortions and deprivations that predatory behaviour produces.

Key personal "skill" for rulers in the cheating process is to keep the general public ignorant of their nature and intentions (Kramer, 2015). As for the social dimension, "advantages" from which the ruler enjoys in this vein vary from country to country.

In the case of Turkey, three main pillars should be recognised as the ones over which the Erdoğanist predatory state rises.

First Pillar: refers to the spiritual power of Islam in hearts and minds. *World Values Survey (2010 – 2014)* indicates that 68.1 % of Turkish respondents give utmost importance to the religion while 24.6 % sees it rather important (WVS, 2015).

Thanks to his "Islamist" (not Islamic) background, Erdoğan ingeniusly associated religious matters with his political agenda and ultimately turned the state and religion into hand and glove. Thus, he resolved the conventional contrast between politics and religion. This also revealed that God and afterlife no longer have any meaning in the corrupted world of the AKP elite despite their apparent belief in both notions. From their viewpoint, Muslim values can be interpreted in the form of "ideology" that is not "religious" as normally understood.

Once fully established, through mass media and other ideological apparatuses like education and religious services led by the Religious Affairs *(Diyanet)* as the head of the religious establishment in Turkey, this understanding ultimately produced an interesting "inversion" among the majority of Turkish citizens: As moral understanding of the religious matters disappears, reliance on interpretation derived from the "pious" discourse of politicians increases.

Diyanet, relying on the political Islamic discourse seeing the "State" *(dawlat)* at the centre of the Faith, ingeniously matched the political/Palatial questions with the existential concerns of believers' everyday life and imparted to the symbols of the nation-state like flag, territory, army, patriotism etc. a religious aura. Friday sermons *(hutbe)* at mosques are of particular importance in this vein.

Therefore, it is unsurprising to see that conservative Turkish citizens tend to *fetishize* the STATE with capital let-

ters by ascribing a kind of divinity to it. Many believe that the state and ruler mirror God; without them, faith ceases to rise and the world collapses. Borrowing from Karl Marx speaking of commodity fetishism in capitalist societies, we could then identify this kind of reification as "state fetishism."[6]

Happenings across the SoE period also reaffirmed that, for many pious citizens, primacy of the state over religious pluralism is the essence of faith. That is why Erdoğan, in fighting with the Gülen sympathisers, has taken wider support from the conservative right-wing, rather than secularists.

Here is the point: this cultural ecology is what makes Erdoğan and others in the core AKP circle pious Muslims, not just the opposite! It is this cultural ecology to encourage Erdoğan, on several occasions, to declare bringing up "pious generations" by promoting state-run religious schools *(imam-hatip)* that had been held limited in number because of secularist concerns. As a striking detail, AKP elites send their kids to secular schools.

It is also this inversion leading the supporters of Erdoğan to believe that he mobilizes his political power to raise the divine flag of Islam, to promote the unity of nation etc. Yet the facts prove the opposite. Thus, "grand corruptions" at the top could be best hidden away from the public eyes by the moral corruption of the religious establishment.

Diyanet, taking charge of AKP's campaign machinery to some extent, works as a conservative authoritarian force acting to mystify asymmetrical power relations and unequal distribution of resources. In a large sense, it derives its authority from some orthodox interpretation of Islamic theology praising obedience to Muslim rulers even if they turn into bloody tyrants.

---

6. Here, I used the term fetish as "an object of religious veneration." For further modern and non-modern usages of the terms fetishism and reification, see Silva (2013).

Turkey's case dramatically demonstrates that, in a society without moral constraints and with low risk of punishment, it is rational for a greedy ruler to act as a shoplifter or looter. A religion comprising rituals and abstract performance of belief, however, it provides little to build a theft deterrent system, but more to produce "pious thieves" as in the case of the reign of Erdoğan.

Consistent with this understanding, AKP elites invoke the religion when it suits them, as on ritual occasions or as a tactic in pursuing a particular agenda, but they also employ it for narrower and more fundamental interests which may lead them to exclude "others" from the brotherhood of believers. Such an antagonistic structure constitutes a vital base which Erdoğan, although he actually acts like a robber, relied on in channelling the flood of wealth into his hands.

As a result, thanks to the exploitation of religious sentiments, they gradually built a system that contains within itself the conditions for its own reproduction. In this process, AKP supporters were not only exploited within "clientelistic" practices but they were also *deformed*. If we forget this result of the system, we will never understand why they cannot be expected to rise up when the regime enters into one of its many economic crises.

It is also Islamism, as combined with the state fetishism, which buys compliance through some display of piety before the public: Turkey's experience within the last decade revealed that the conservative majority may tend to surrender their will to the state just as the ruling elite appears sensitive to the religious matters like *headcraft* of women, building monumental mosques most of which are empty in praying times, inaugurating religious schools, etc.

Last but not least, what we should have learned from the last decade of Turkey under the AKP governments is that, as an ideology, "Islamism" is a threat to the peace and tolerance promoted by Islam itself. It rather works in a way to produce political "principles" from the religious substance. All the available evidence makes it clear that, contrary to the secularist fears, the AKP never aimed to "Islamicise" the society and/or state, but rather to convert people from being constitutional citizens into herds of subjects through Islamist antagonism.

Therefore, it is fair to conclude that the AKP cannot be seen as a centre-right party like *Christian Democratic* parties in Europe, but is best seen as akin to a party with "authoritarian-predatory" features characterised by the use of violence and patronage like the "Zimbabwe National Union-Patriotic Front" (ZANU-PF) of Mugabe.

Second Pillar: refers to a political economy that couples high growth rates with persistent poverty. As Robinson (1999) suggested, even self-serving regimes would have an incentive to promote development if they could extract enough of the resulting wealth. It was true that the AKP, particularly in its first term in the office, achieved relatively high rates of growth and at the same time prevented poor from becoming independent in the sense of financial well-being.

This performance in the past, to a large extent, explains the underlying logic of the "Electoral Authoritarianism" (EA) in today's Turkey: increasing evidence reveals that EA regimes typically construct their electoral coalitions around the poor, who are more cheaply co-opted. As Miller (2017) simply put it, the poor voters, reversing the democratic pattern, are the most likely to vote in autocratic elections and often tend to support the ruling party, AKP in Turkey.

Thus, Erdoğan guaranteed himself an electoral base and manpower for his Islamist ideology. That is especially the case for poor voters who are more willing to compromise their ideology for immediate private consumption. What Erdoğan and the AKP elite have learned from running the Turkish economy was that "higher incomes reduce the grip and cost effectiveness of clientelism" as both personal wealth and local development reduce individuals' willingness to sell his/her vote (Miller, 2017).

By the way, removal of the "Bulletin of the Social Assistance Statistics of Turkey" from publication as of 2014 seems to be significant before such a veneer of growth in figures. Factual poverty inventories indicating cliental relations between poor and incumbent have therefore remained inaccessible since then. *(See figure 8, page 223)*

Yet TÜİK (TURKSTAT) statistics, despite prevalent distortions in the methodology, may give an overall insight into living conditions: as of 2016, 14.3 % of the population (appr. 12 million) lives below the national poverty line while 68 % of the population are indebted.[7] This, more or less, clarifies why the number of citizens whose General Health Insurance premium is being born by the state totalled a little less than 6.7 million in 2016 according to the Ministry of Family and Social Policies.[8]

Apparently, at least half of the population has been made dependants by a policy leaving the nation in the "middle-income trap" and even addictive of social assistances: Not fighting against poverty, but making it a standing form of life for a vast majority of the masses while the returns of growth are gathered by the top end of the distribution pyramid. This provides the AKP with keen voters from low-income social classes as represented by

---

7. http://www.tuik.gov.tr/PreHaberBultenleri.do?id=24579 (Accessed: 5 February 2018).
8. Annual Activity Report-2016: https://sgb.aile.gov.tr/uploads/pages/arge-raporlar/2016-yili-faaliyet-raporu.pdf (Accessed: 5 August 2018). By the way, with the Presidential Decree no.1 of 10th July 2018, this Ministry was merged with the Ministry of Labour and Social Security under the title of the "Ministry of Family, Labour and Social Services."

1. *those who shrouded in white cloths (kefen in Islamic tradition, to shroud dead before being buried) symbolising that they are committed to go as far as sacrificing themselves for Erdoğan, and*

2. *the emergence of pro-Erdoğan paramilitary groupings akin to Esquadřao da Morte (death squads) of Latin America in the 1970 s.*

Although very little is known about why the poor vote for such a system keeping them in that way, Kurer (2001) underlines the interactions between poverty and "risk aversion": as poor's income is close to subsistence, any decrease threatens their survival. They can then insure themselves against this risk by joining clientele networks as the leader provides "subsistence insurance". The cost of this insurance is the diminished income that accompanies corruption.

Such an interaction accounts why corruption tends to increase under the Erdoğan regime. By various years, the "Corruption Perception Index" (CPI) of Transparency International[9] ranks Turkey with the following figures (Table 4).

Table 4: Turkey in the Corruption Perception Indexes (2010 – 2017)

Years	Ranking (out of Countries)	Countries with the Same Rank
2010	56/178	Namibia, Malaysia
2011	61/182	Cuba, Latvia
2012	54/174	Malaysia, Latvia, Czech Republic
2013	53/175	Malaysia
2014	64/174	Oman, Macedonia
2015	66/167	Sao Tome & Principe, Macedonia
2016	75/176	Bulgaria, Kuwait, Tunisia
2017	81/180	Ghana, India, Morocco

Data Source: Transparency International CPIs

9. CPI: https://www.transparency.org/research/cpi/overview (Accessed: 6 August 2018).

The rankings reveal a country status evolving steadily from bad to worst and indicate a serious corruption problem. Nevertheless, in the recent elections this trend had little effect on voting behaviours. Since the costs of corruption are born by the nation as a whole, the members' share of the costs will be less than their gains (Kurer, 2001).

Yet poverty alone is not sufficient enough to explain the predatory voting behaviour. At least for Turkey, as well as the cultural ecology that enables the politicians to exploit the religious sentiments; this account needs to be considered as coupled with the corruption in the society.

Third Pillar: refers to distinctive conditions of Turkish society: so, when they came to power, Erdoğan and his associates saw a less-educated, divided society as key to maintaining their predatory goals over the country.

They also correctly ascertained that, as society becomes more polarised, the marginal returns for increasing polarisation increase to their advantage. When Erdoğan took position concerning the high-profile trials involving hundreds of arrests like *"Ergenekon"* (Turkish Gladio), *"Balyoz"* (coup plan), and "KCK" (urban wing of PKK), as well as maintaining his personal rule over the state and society, the ultimate goal was to deepen the polarization in question.

Today, Erdoğan's AKP rules a country where society is highly fragmented and deeply polarized. Yet this polarization goes beyond the "right" and "left" traditions of the political divide, and rather involves different Islamist and Nationalist groups, secularists, leftist-socialist, liberals, Kurds, Alevis, and so forth. Such a fragmentation therefore disallows the rise of "social movements" taking place "as conversations – not as solo performances but as interactions among parties", as C. Tilly (1998) identified.

They traditionally interact less and distrust each other more while the attention, to a large extent, is directed to the exclusive control of the state apparatuses and its benefits e. g. concessions, public procurements, official positions of authority, etc. Apart from the historical legacy that has still remained prevalent in governing the state, one underlying reason must be the following: they heavily suffer from "fundraising" simply because modern forms of "gift-giving" are less common among Turks.

That is what the AKP governments have better profited from for personal gains of Erdoğan. So, their interactions with the political top don't create a bargain "between" equals, but rather a hierarchical giver-taker relation, and ultimately make takers vulnerable to the influence of the state. The ruler, may find a way to penetrate deep into society to control ordinary citizens and even opposition if he feeds and fuels them towards his political agenda.

Increasing evidence shows that Erdoğan has achieved to gather all right-wing segments including political parties and religious groups in his camp this way. He (or his strategists) was also well aware that a communication strategy with respect to public opinion offers considerable potential in order to help sustain such a political gathering and to brutalise remaining opponents politically. This strategy encompasses

1. *praising a past greatness that never was, giving a right-wing populist response to the political conditions, and promoting a combined use of a Nationalist-Islamist narrative with vulgar, uncivil tones, and*

2. *creating a domestic scapegoat enemy, directing social hatred to this enemy through mass media, and finally*

the witch-hunt of this scapegoat initiated by the state security apparatus.

The conditions that have been experienced by the followers of the "Gülen Movement" suit best to the latter: as a result of media campaign accompanied by mass arrests and dismissals under the siege of the allegations concerning the coup attempt of 15 July 2016 both secular and conservative segments with radically different goals joined his alliance against this movement, even though they know that Erdoğan's outcry against Gülen sympathisers is a smoke-screen for the real coup to legalise predatory operations.

Since a multi-polar structure with those traits is devoid of plurality and further leads to a cultural ecology in which a "civil society" can't possibly take root, the groupings concerned cannot easily evolve into "social movements". And ultimately, less room remains for a consensus or compromise in the political realm.

Not coincidentally, when they achieved to break this barrier through the network of schools and charity organizations, Erdoğan accused the followers of the Gülen Movement of being "a state within the state" and eventually plotting to overthrow the government. Namely, to some extent, this group appears to be a victim of its own success. Despite various reasons spoken before the media, from the vantage point of Erdoğan, Gülen sympathisers seem to use the schooling and charity network at global level to avoid being incorporated into an Islamist ideology that puts religious values in service of his political agenda.

The degree of the polarization can also be traced from internationally recognized sources. For example, just 11.6 % of Turkish respondents, according to the World Values Survey

(2010 – 2014), say that most people can be trusted while 82.9 % say one needs to be very careful in dealing with people (wvs, 2015). This implies their "fear" of one another is great and that they are ready to exclude one another while each one is seeking to control the state. That is a society in which nobody does anything for the common good.

Furthermore, polarization generally promotes collective violence because it makes the "us-them" boundary more salient, hollows out the uncommitted middle, intensifies conflicts across the boundary, raises the stakes of winning or losing, and enhances opportunities for leaders to initiate action against their enemies (Tilly, 2003). Such was experienced in the course of the *Gezi Park* protests in June 2013 and more visibly during the coup attempt of 15 July.

Under these circumstances, it is not surprising to see that Erdoğan's campaign against disloyal groups like the Gülen Movement, the Kurds, socialists etc. gathered broad support from voters. As the notable political figures chose to endorse his correctness (!) in that respect, the political opposition remained loose and loyal to some extent. That is also the case in the "war on terror" waged by Erdoğan in regards to the instability in Syria.

Today, in persecution of dissents, Erdoğan not only relies on the SoE regime, but rather on the polarisation within the society in political/cultural terms. That was the case when the absolute majority of the voters (51.4 %), with a turnout of 85 %, endorsed the constitutional amendments of 16 April 2017. It is also reaffirmed that, although the controversial numbers of the votes for "Yes" represent a narrower margin of victory than he expected, the largest of these fragments are firmly in favour of granting Erdoğan dictatorial powers.

As a result, if we accurately identify those conceptual pillars, we then understand how Erdoğan and his allies still remain in the political theatre as leading players even under the following conditions:

a. *routinely prolonged SoE and rule by decrees scaring both foreign and local investors,*

b. *the country's growing diplomatic isolation marked by Erdoğan's personal zigzags,*

c. *the loss of qualified officials aggravating the bureaucratic performance in public services, resulting in a decrease in societal trust,*

d. *significant delays in fulfilment of the promises he made to the voters in order to win his referendum in 2017 and snap the elections on 24 June 2018.*

CONCLUSION: CULTIVATING THE CORRUPTION IN SOCIETY

Turkey became increasingly predatory under the Erdoğan-led governments, in part due to the dynamics in society, economy, and the state. The key word in any analysis of the Erdoğan regime is "predatory" because the term "corruption" has remained deficient to describe the affairs since the failed coup of 15 July. He legitimized the robbery and plundering of national/private wealth through an ideological discourse highlighting the necessary duty of the state and incumbent to defend the Faith and to promote the variety of associated activities which this entailed.

What we have learned from the happenings throughout his reign is that, (1) researchers no longer have a chance to assume the electorate as a check on predatory operations of rulers even if they know about it, and (2) we are mistaken if we think that a majority will save us from greedy leaders like Erdoğan.

As a conclusion of this paper, without jumping into a mega-analysis concerning the possible lifetime of Erdoğan at the Palace (it is being highly debated in other media), we suggest to study the roots of the predatory voting behaviour in Turkish society, and to seek answers to the following questions:

1. *How can such a moral bankruptcy influence huge parts of society?*

2. *How can a political leadership cultivate corruption in society instead of challenging it?*

3. *How and why do individuals remain unconcerned and even tolerant when rulers regularly extract resources from the national economy in a largely predatory manner?*

Thus, we could likely develop a long-term exit strategy with a focus on teaching our children, as argued by Kramer (2015), "to recognize the early warning signs of predators who may seduce, con, exploit, or abuse them." That is of paramount importance for social scientists including anthropologists unless their qualifications lean more towards ideological loyalty than academic skills.

CHAPTER SEVEN

ECtHR: a new solution partner of the Erdoğan regime?*

* The initial version of this chapter first appeared as an article on the PPJ website on 19.6.2017.

> *The "perfect crime" does not consist in killing the victim or the witnesses, but rather in obtaining the silence of the witnesses, the deafness of the judges, and the inconsistency of the testimony.*
>
> Jean-François Lyotard

BURNING HERETICS WITH LOW COST

ALL THE DOORS ARE BEING CLOSED IN THEIR FACES. This may suit best to describe the harsh conditions under which victims of the "state of emergency" (SoE) lived in Turkey. According to the Turkish Constitution, in case of the SoE, the government is allowed to introduce "decree laws" (governmental decrees with the force of law) in order to recover normal conditions. The Turkish Constitution also stipulates that decree laws cannot be brought before the courts or be reviewed by the Constitutional Court (AYM) both in procedural and substantial terms.

Therefore Erdoğan, from his point of view, is fully right when he sees the coup attempt of 15 July 2016 as *Dei Gratia* (a gift from God). This attempt whose major perpetrators still remain in darkness was the apparent reason of the SoE. Happenings since then showed that, in his vocabulary, Dei Gratia means: "I use the coup as a convenient excuse to wage a war against dissents."

Relying on this blanked cheque, the Erdoğan regime started

to dismiss thousands of civil servants right after the coup attempt through a series of decree laws with a blacklist of those labelled as FETO-linked terrorists.

By the way, FETO, an acronym of "Fethullahist Terror Organisation" has been made popular by the regime in Turkey. However, the group was recognized by the EU Commission as "Gülen Movement" in the Turkey Progress Report of 9 November 2016 while British parliament, in its report on the relations with Turkey (FAC, 2017), used the term *Gülenists*. By any means, the international community has not stigmatized this movement as a terrorist organisation.

Table 5: Dismissals and Reinstates by Decree Laws (2016 – 2018)

	Decree Laws		# of Dismissals	Reinstated
	No	Date		
1	668	27 July 2016	1.684	0
2	669	31 July 2016	1.389	0
3	670	17 Aug 2016	2.692	0
4	672	01 Sept 2016	50.684	0
5	675	29 Oct. 2016	10.129	74
6	677	22 Nov. 2016	15.653	155
7	679	06 Jan. 2017	8.400	277
8	683	23 Jan. 2017	367	124
9	686	07 Feb. 2017	1.464	17
10	688	20 March 2017	0	420
11	689	29 April 2017	3.974	236
12	692	14 July 2017	7.563	312
13	693	25 Aug. 2017	928	57
14	695	24 Dec. 2017	2.765	115
15	697	12 Jan. 2018	262	1.823
16	701	08 July 2018	18.632	148
	Total		129.586	3.758

Data Source: Turkish Official Gazette

The numbers of victims are getting higher and higher every day. The Erdoğan regime introduced a very practical (!) solution to make the victimization process easy for civil servants: ready-made blacklists are appended to the standard cabinet decrees and published on the website of the Official Gazette. In this way, with the 16 decree laws, totally 129.586 civil servants have been fired (Table 5). All of these decrees – in various dates – were subsequently adopted by the Parliament.

Note that the figures above only include dismissals by decree laws. The dismissals of judges and prosecutors, for example, are decided by the Council of Judges and Prosecutors (HSK) with ad hoc judicial decrees (Table 6).

Table 6: Dismissal of the Judges and Prosecutors by HSK (2016–2017)

	HSK Decision		Official Gazette		# of
	Date	No.	Date	No.	Dismissals
1	24 Aug 2016	2016/426	25 Aug 2016	29812	2.847
2	31 Aug. 2016	2016/428	3 Sept. 2016	29820	543
3	4 Oct. 2016	2016/430	6 Oct. 2016	29849	430
4	15 Nov. 2016	2016/440	17 Nov. 2016	29891	440
5	13 Feb. 2017	2017/35	21 Feb. 2017	29986	227
6	17 Mar. 2017	2017/113	18 Mar. 2017	30011	202
7	3 April 2017	2017/665	4 April 2017	30028	45
8	5 May 2017	2017/682	6 May 2017	30058	107
9	5 Oct. 2017	2017/770	6 Oct. 2017	30202	39
	Total				4.279

Data Source: Turkish Official Gazette, HSK website

The general board of the Turkish Constitution Court (AYM), on 4 August 2016, decided to remove two of its own members from the office on the basis of the "social environment intelligence" and the "opinion" (*kanaat* in Turkish) constituted by the majority of the remaining members.[1] In addition to this, the AYM dismissed 41 of its officials on 30 December 2016 with the allegation of their ties to the Gülen Movement.

Together with the other arbitrary dismissals by public authorities on the basis of the Decree Law no. 667, by the state

---

1. Without going into other peculiarities, this decision reveals that AYM values individual opinions of its members over the principles promoted by both the Turkish Constitution and the ECHR. The decision in question can be downloaded from http://www.kararlaryeni.anayasa.gov.tr/Karar/Content/717f7c20-b696-4379-84f6-dfb5 68f8844 a? exclude Gerekce = False & words Only = False (26 October 2018).

enterprises, and so forth, the grand total is –conservatively – estimated to go near 170.000. In any case, dismissals from public account for about 7 % of the total number of civil servants, 2.4 million as of July 2016.² I call this **"Bureaucra-cide"** so as to identify the politically-organised, massive and cruel character of the practice.

Furthermore, none of these numbers takes into consideration the joblessness in private sector driven by the mass forfeitures and shutting down of the schools, universities, hospitals, media outlets, companies, and so forth. OHCHR (2018), with reference to the government-owned Anadolu Agency (AA), reports that "an additional 22.474 people lost their jobs due to the closure of private institutions for alleged support to the Gülen-network, especially academics, teachers and other staff working in private education institutions" (para.64).³

By the way, the Erdoğan regime, with reference to the "suspension" procedure, propagates that 40.000 civil servants were reinstated and this lying even took place within the EU Progress Report (European Commission, 2018: 4) for Turkey: "Since the introduction of the SoE, over 150.000 people were taken into custody, 78.000 were arrested and over 110.000 civil servants were dismissed whilst, according to the authorities, some 40.000 were reinstated of which some 3.600 by decree" (emphasis added). I suppose this must have been caused by dishonesty of the Erdoğan regime which increasingly relied upon lies and hoaxes in both domestic and international arenas, as well as

---

2. A statistical circular by the Ministry of Labour and Social Security gives the total number of civil servants as of July 2016: 2.452.249 (4 July 2016 dated Official Gazette with no. 29 762).
3. However, we could not find this exact figure in the referenced booklet of the AA, "*Democracy Triumphs in Turkey:* FETO's *Coup Attempt in Turkey, A Timeline*, 15 July 2016," available at http: //aa. com. tr/uploads/TempUserFiles/FETO_coup_ENG. pdf (Accessed: 26 11. 2018). Reference seems to be irrelevant to the content.

assuming that the EU services might not be aware of the meaning of these terms in the Turkish legal framework.[4]

According to the Turkish Code of Civil Servants no. 657, suspension does not have the same effects as the dismissal that ends the civil servant status. Suspension is a disciplinary measure for civil servants when they are under investigation prohibiting them from official duties as well as access to their office for the safety of the investigation. In this period with a maximum of three months, civil servants are paid two thirds of their salaries as they are still civil servants.

If the investigation report requires the person to be sanctioned with dismissal, the relevant authority then turns the suspension to a dismissal which is open to judicial review. In lack of substantially maintained misconduct, the suspension ends and the person returns back to office. The dismissal by a decree law, however, is to leave no safety margin to civil servants such as in-house investigation or judicial remedy. Therefore, the phrases reinstate of 40.000 officials refer to the removal of their suspension. At present, thoese dismissals can only be removed by the "SoE Inquiry Commission" (see below).

Turning to the main issue, not only being dismissed but also lifelong banishment from public positions, invalidation of licenses and diplomas proving vocational qualifications, cancellation of passports were put into force without any interrogation, judicial decision, and further procedures. Thus, civil servants, stigmatized by the specific decrees, have become "jobless-with-no-qualification" with hardly very few employers who might still wish to employ such people if any.

---

4. A diplomatic note arguing that "31.000 civil servants had been reinstated after their cases were investigated" was also delivered by the Turkish Embassy in London to the parliamentary Foreign Affairs Committee (FAC) and this lying was included into the report on "The UK's Relations with Turkey" (FAC, 2017: 45).

CONTROVERSIES IN THE JUDICIAL SYSTEM

On 2 October 2016, contrary to its previous position, the AYM refused to review the decree laws in terms of constitutionality because they were introduced based on the SoE.[5] On the other hand, the Constitution reckons decree laws as "laws" to be adopted by the Parliament (once published they have to be submitted to the approval of the parliament). In its opinion, the review of decree laws rests with the Parliament only, and therefore they cannot be considered usual administrative measures and thus remain out of jurisprudence of the AYM itself and of the Supreme Administrative Court (Council of State) and local administrative courts.

As for the individual petitions, i. e. the ultimate domestic remedy before the ECtHR, with reference to the article 45(3) of Law no. 6216 on the "Establishment and Judicial Procedures of the Constitutional Court," the AYM reckons itself unauthorized to review individual petitions against the "legislative actions" and "regulatory administrative actions." That was the case in its 30 11. 2015 dated decision concerning the individual petitions of the rapporteurs dismissed by Law no. 6524 concerning the [High] Council of Judges and Prosecutors (HSK).[6] This implies that the same would be the case for the applications lodged by the victims of decree laws unless some extraordinary change emerges in the political sphere of Turkey.

Evidently, in its judgment of 4 November 2016, the 5th Chamber of the Supreme Administrative Court (in charge of

---

5. The AYM decision was published in the Official Gazette of **8 October 2016, with no. 29 882.**
6. Not "High" anymore. Following the referendum of 16 April 2017 concerning the constitutional amendments, the Council lost its high status.

reviewing Cabinet Decrees) decided that compliance of decree laws goes beyond its jurisdiction and should be examined by the first-instance administrative courts.

Against this, almost all the local administrative courts started to reject the files without examination, even with the same wordings: "decree laws are legislative not administrative and we are not authorized to examine their compliance." Namely, those dismissals fall outside their remit! Independent observers may check it: no contrary decision has been issued yet.

A very lawful entrapment in the full sense of the word! Ingenius (!) interpretations by the top agents of the judicial branch, creating a vague area out of any legal boundaries, systematically yield nothing to be done for the citizens who are legally killed (see the term "civil death" in chapter 4) by the government. Indeed, that it be a joke for them, so there is no court to hear and they are unworthy of a fair trial or access to court.

Worse still, they are not even worthy of an official one-page notice. Practicality prevails! That is why the government listed their names within the Official Gazette and announced that these people were fired as they are linked with "terrorist organisations" and "entities or groups" which are considered harmful to the national security.

That is all! No need to occupy the courts, no need to waste any paper on them!

However, neither the Government nor the MGK has disclosed the names of these organisations, entities or groups. No need; be practical, just refer to FETO with a political rhetoric.

JUDICIAL INNOVATION: A NON-JUDICIAL COMMISSION

As a political response to the voices raised by the international community reactions, with the Decree Law no. 685 dated 23 1. 2017, the Erdoğan regime formed the "State of Emergency Inquiry Commission" (hereafter "the Commission"), a non-judicial entity, which would have the task of adjudicating upon appeals against the "measures" taken by decree laws issued in the context of the SoE, including the dismissals of civil servants.

In one hand, that was just to waste the victims' time and to create an appearance of fairness as well as respecting the proposals made by the Secretary General of the CoE[7] and the Venice Commission (2016) in its Opinion no. 865/2016: "creation of an independent *ad hoc* body for the examination of individual cases of dismissals, subject to subsequent judicial review" (para. 228). It is everyone's secret that the Commission's establishment was purely to prevent the ECtHR from taking jurisdiction for claims in another hand.

Yet the Commission with its seven members (yes, 7 in figures!), in lack of any deadline for making its decisions, will decide on whether thousands of dismissals are right or wrong. That is fine, despite the fact that its members are appointed among senior officials by the Prime Minister (PM) [who is no longer exists], Minister of Interior, and Minister of Justice, namely by the same leading political actors behind the mass dismissals. Then, there is no reason to believe that it would not be *independent* of providing appropriate (!) redress for the victims' complaints as recommended by the Venice Commission (2016):

> *This body should be independent, impartial and be given sufficient*

---

7. CoE Press Release dated 9 December 2016: https://rm.coe.int/168071f1d7 (Accessed: 19 June 2017).

powers to restore the status quo ante, and/or, where appropriate, to provide adequate compensation (para. 222).

OK, but what about the administrative courts? What are they supposed to do when the Commission takes the ground? Or, would the Commission function as a semi-court parallel to the courts? No, do not worry. Thanks to the provisions of the Decree Law no. 690 dated 29 April 2017 which was complimentary to the 685, the regime actually put an end to this "controversy": according to the article 56 of the Decree Law, if any citizen lodges an application to examine his/her dismissal, the courts, without taking any decision on the matter, are obliged to transfer the file to the Commission directly.

Thus, seven supermen will be expected to perform magical work in regards to hundreds of thousands of complaints whereas hundreds of judges spend time on holiday.[8] That is to say, **courts are disallowed to examine dismissals by the decree laws. No controversy, so no judicial remedy. [N. B. not only dismissals but also the measures listed in article 2(1) of Decree Law no. 685 such as closing down of universities, schools, associations, media outlets etc. will be reviewed upon appeal to the Commission].**

Of course, decisions of the Commission remain subject to judicial review. But this jurisdiction is only limited to the decisions taken by the Commission itself and cannot be extended to the actual subject of violation, i. e. eligibility of decree laws as well as accountability of the regime in wrongdoings.

Worse still, let us say, had you brought its decision before the court, article 55 of Decree Law no. 690 stipulates that neither the

---

8. The Commission reports that, as of 22 June 2018, 21.500 out of 108.905 applications in total were concluded whereas 87.405 files are still pending. https://ohalkomisyonu.basbakanlik.gov.tr/duyurular (Accessed: 22 June 2018).

Commission nor the Prime Ministry can be designated as the "respondent". Instead, the procedure is addressed automatically to "the institution applicant last served before dismissal." The Decree Law handles all judicial matters quite in detail in the tone of "instructions to the judges".

No surprise, such is not a matter of concern in today's Turkey, as Erdoğan and his ministers (nobody else!) frequently declare that judges are independent in their decisions.

From scratch, it was crystal clear for us that the Commission, as such, would not and cannot provide a real avenue for accountability for the regime and proper redress for the victims. So, it cannot be regarded as victim-centred but a political project.[9] Therefore, the impetus for accountability should have come from the international or supranational structures like the ECtHR.

AT THE GATE OF THE ECtHR

Under these circumstances the victims of the decree laws naturally turn their attention to the ECtHR. Since the occurrence of the first dismissals in September of 2016, thousands of appeals have accumulated at the register of the ECtHR, more than 30.000 as of 31 December 2017 (see below). This figure representing mass violations of human rights in Turkey turned a test-case measuring commitment of the ECtHR to its main principles that have been prevailed so far. Let us have a look how the ECtHR has dealt with this challenge. *(See figure 9, page 224)*

Indeed, it may be easy to review some one-off violation for the ECtHR or even the Chambers may order the joinder of appli-

---

9. Amnesty International (2018), in its brief report on the case, also found wide range of examples of inefficiencies associated to the Commission's *modus operandi*, while OHCHR (2018) concludes that the Commission cannot be considered as an independent body that will guarantee full respect of due process (para.108).

cations with similar content. But this time, the case seems to be the first in its history: applications concerning human rights violations with highly collective character. Therefore, it might be inevitable for the ECtHR to apply a "pilot case" procedure to cater for the ever-increasing wave of applications concerning similar issues that arise from nonconformity of domestic law (decree laws in the case of Turkey) with the European Convention on Human Rights (ECHR).

Besides, the ideal approach is that each and every one of its judgments should be a "pilot" which means that the respondent party and effectively all other High Contracting Parties should amend their practice to be in compliance with the ECHR (Dzehtsiarou and Greene, 2011). Such would also be the best way to answer the common interest of Turkish applicants in a timely manner.

Instead, the ECtHR preferred a third way. It took one of the files and found it "inadmissible". That was the decision *Zihni v. Turkey* (59 061/16), of 8 December 2016, referring to the principle of "exhaustion of domestic remedies". We might fully agree with this procedural point of view, so it is the norm, and domestic courts should play their role in the ECHR protection system, at least in procedural sense.

The system concerned works with a very basic principle: a constitutional Europe should first be rooted in the member states, e. g. Turkey. That is not only for keeping the ECtHR away from the challenges, but also for setting a platform facilitating fact-oriented analyses in which the judges make a lot of work of the circumstances of the case. Otherwise, the ECtHR may turn to a first-instance court due to the direct flow of applications from all member countries.

As far as individual petitions to the AYM are concerned, in principle the ECtHR deals with the applications which exhausted this final domestic remedy only. Taking into consideration of the fact that the AYM had not yet ruled on whether it had jurisdiction to examine those appeals, in *Zihni v. Turkey*, the ECtHR kindly made a distinction between

1. *"ruling on the constitutionality of a law in the context of a challenge to constitutionality"* and

2. *"reviewing specific decisions taken in application of the provisions of that particular law."*

It is still unknown for us whether the AYM would show such a kindness.

The ECtHR is fully correct at that point: when constitutionality is acknowledged by the AYM, this does not prevent members of the public from lodging an individual appeal before it. But contrary to this, such may prevent the AYM from reviewing these appeals for the sake of being "consistent" (if it is still something desirable) as well as the above-mentioned restriction in article 45(3) of Law no. 6216.

The decision *Zihni v. Turkey* also revealed that the ECtHR is well aware of the controversies in the Turkish constitutional/legal framework and values the position of the AYM concerning thousands of individual petitions which had been lodged against dismissals by decree laws. This implies that the final position of the ECtHR would be very dependent on the position to be adopted by the AYM in these files.

Thanks to *Köksal v. Turkey* (70 478/16), we found a semi-final position on the matter. In this decision dated 12 June 2017, the ECtHR dismissed the application for failure to exhaust domestic remedies, finding that Mr. Köksal had to use the remedy provided for under Decree Law no. 685 i. e. "the Commission".

However, Mr. Köksal lodged his application on 4 November 2016, long before the introduction of Decree Law no. 685, 23 1. 2017. Relying on the approach adopted in the decision *Zihni v. Turkey*, Mr. Köksal should have only been required to exhaust the following domestic remedies: the administrative court, Supreme Administrative Court (of appeal) and AYM respectively.

From the details of this decision, we understand that the ECtHR is well aware of this condition.

Then, what is the reason leading the ECtHR to make such an exemption? Why did the ECtHR point to a remedy not yet in existence at that time? The Court itself answers: *"to test the limits of this new remedy for the victim of an alleged Convention violation".*

"To test the limits of the remedy..." Given that it remains unknown for us how and when this occurs, how should we interpret this novelty in the sense of jurisprudence?

Although both Decree Laws no. 685 and no. 690 clearly indicate the limits of this new remedy, the ECtHR deems necessary to test it! Then, if Mr. Köksal and others agree to be a "tester", that will be the first testing initiative in the judicial sector. No joke, the ECtHR has the image of a serious entity even though we have not found any decision in this respect.

ERDOĞAN'S REMEDY BAPTISED BY THE ECTHR!

This decision also reveals that the ECtHR, with reference to the opinion of Venice Commission, appreciates the establishment of the Commission and recognizes it as a competent authority although it cheats the roles of the courts in adjudicating upon appeals against dismissals. The ECtHR also considers that, with this measure, Turkish government put an end *"to the controversy about the jurisdiction of the national courts as regards the judicial review of measures taken under legislative decrees issued during a state of emergency and had designated the administrative courts to hear administrative appeals against the commission's decisions."*

Fully correct! No controversy remained. How is that possible? Let us analyse the quotation.

1. As mentioned above, national courts are no longer authorized for the judicial review of measures taken under decree laws. Indeed, this provision is fully compliant with the recent decisions of the local administrative courts on the basis of the lack of authorization.

2. Administrative courts are authorised only to hear administrative appeals against the Commission's decisions, not against the decree laws of the Cabinet. Thus, the government, in a tricky way, achieved to move decree laws out of judicial review.

And the ECtHR, despite its reference to *"a possible re-examination of the question of the effectiveness and reality of the remedy"*, appreciates these outcomes of measures taken by the Erdoğan regime for the sake of "fairness". Such a re-examination however can only be possible when Mr. Zihni and Mr. Köksal exhausted all domestic remedies including the Commission unless of course a new remedy is introduced meanwhile.

From the details of *Köksal v. Turkey*, it could be noticed that Mr. Köksal did not exhaust any of the domestic remedies including the individual petition to the AYM. However, instead of making a general reference to the principle of exhaustion of domestic remedies in its inadmissibility decision, the ECtHR preferred to recognize the Commission set up by the government. This implies that high judges had come together just to honour this Commission through the application of Mr. Köksal.

Now, what shall Mr. Köksal and Mr. Zihni do? They will turn back to ground zero of their dismissal. They will travel over a long distance from the Commission to the ECtHR, final destination. Anyway, they have enough time to deal with such affairs.

What shall the ECtHR members do in the meantime? Of course, the ECtHR left the door open to the possibility of further evaluation of the remedy in question at a later date. Be that as it may, not earlier than five years, they will be able to test the effectiveness of this new "remedy".

The pending applications will therefore be treated as *inadmissible* by a single judge in line with the decision *Köksal v. Turkey*. Thus, they will save time to deal with other human rights violations. Moreover, the ECtHR declared 30.000 applications concerning the post-coup measures inadmissible between mid-June and 31 December 2017.[10]

What shall Erdoğan and his supporters do? They will likely feel free to publish new lists of dismissals and to persecute dissenters. Fortunately, victims have an "accessible remedy" to appeal, the Commission which was baptised by the ECtHR!

CRITICISM AND COE RESPONSE

Of course, the ECtHR does not work in isolation and conservative interpretations may be understood to some extent

---

10. CoE Statement: https://www.coe.int/en/web/portal/-/council-of-europe-meeting-with-the-media-and-law-studies-association-turkey- (Accessed: 5 August 2018).

when the national authorities acted carefully taking into consideration proper administrative and judicial safeguards. But, as the overwhelming evidence showed, such is not the case in today's Turkey.

The *Köksal v. Turkey* decision triggered considerable criticism of the ECtHR. Many complained that the reticence of the ECtHR to accept claims overlooked the reality that the Turkish justice system was unable and/or unwilling to provide effective remedies. This led responsible law associations to organise a conference held on 5 March 2018 in Germany bringing together leading commentators from across Europe including 70 lawyers, judges, NGO representatives, and academics: *Turkey and the ECtHR: (In)effective Remedies from Strasbourg* (DAV, 2018).

The conference participants discussed the question of whether the Court is providing appropriate remedies to Turkish citizens who have suffered violations of their rights since the abortive coup of July 2016. Final remarks highlighted that

1. *in the case of repetitive violations and intolerance, the Court could decide to absolve applicants from exhaustion of the domestic remedies condition.*

2. *failure of the Court to protect founding values may cause a greater damage to the reputation of the Court.*

One of the closing remarks by the conference moderator, Tony Fisher, Chair of the Human Rights Committee at the Law Society of England and Wales, however, best represents the primacy of the practicality over judicial review of human rights violations: *"the dam will break" when the* ECtHR *may be forced to re-evaluate, and recognize that domestic remedies were no longer effective.*

On the other hand, criticism was not limited to *Köksal v. Turkey* decision that virtually became a reference to treat thousands of applications inadmissible. There are also other instances of the ECtHR failing to provide justice for post-coup victims (Spencer, 2018). For example, in *Bora v. Turkey* (30 647/17) in which the applicant with some serious health problems was kept in pre-trial solitary confinement without justification, the ECtHR, on 21 December 2017, decided that article 3 of the ECHR that prohibits torture and inhuman or degrading treatment had not been violated. Decision implies that Turkish authorities violating human rights may feel free to torture and inhuman practices with impunity.

CoE, first showed a reaction with an uncivil tone. Daniel Holtgen (2018), CoE spokesperson, rebuffed via Twitter: *Criticism of the European Court of Human Rights' handling of Turkish post-coup cases is ill-informed and counterproductive. The ECtHR will not be pressurised by anyone. [...]*. But, three weeks later, he met with the Turkish representatives from the "Media and Law Studies Association" (Spencer, 2018).

Subsequent to the meeting in Strasbourg, on 13 June 2018, the CoE released a statement declaring it is "aware of a common perception among NGOs that the ECtHR is not giving adequate attention to human rights issues in Turkey, but believes this is based on a lack of information and misconceptions." And this statement reiterates the adopted position: "The ECtHR may only deal with cases after all national legal remedies have been exhausted. [...] The ECtHR reserves the right to examine the effectiveness of national legal remedies [...]."

We all are well aware of the fact that the ECtHR's case law is developed on a case-by-case basis with the strict interpretation against the expansion of the ECHR rules outside of the text of the ECHR. However, special consideration should also be given to the fact that "a judgment is legitimate if it is persuasive to the civic society constituted by the ECtHR, and perceived as authoritative by the subjects affected by the ECtHR's decision" (Dzehtsiarou and Greene, 2011).

One last point here: While the CoE made this statement in Strasbourg, human right violations in Turkey continue on a massive scale, with no sign of stopping now (24 June 2018) that Erdoğan has been re-elected. Therefore the ECtHR, if it remains silent, even a kind of "adviser" to the regime, will also continue to receive both applications and criticism.

CROSSING THE RED SEA

We hope the ECtHR is also well aware what Turkish victims are in pursuit of is not only an immediate recovery of their losses but also a strong message to the Erdoğan regime in Turkey. Sometimes political figures, media organs and even civil society may choose to remain silent for some reason which is "politically correct". Under such circumstances, it is the court houses providing an "exposed ground" to walk on for those who escape from persecution.

With reference to a well-known biblical/Qur'anic narrative, let us make an analogy to picture their stress: they have to cross the Red Sea before being exterminated by the Pharaoh and his army. Yes, judges may not part the Red Sea but, at least, may put a halt to persecutions provoked by pharaohs of today like Erdoğan of Turkey.

The *Köksal v. Turkey* decision revealed that the ECtHR is not ready to face such a challenge. Maybe for the first time in the history of the ECtHR, the honour of high judges is at stake. They have unanimously chosen to be "practical" as the Turkish government is and turned out to be the solution partner of the Erdoğan regime in the persecution of dissenters.

CHAPTER EIGHT

Rule-with-violence: Emergence of the erdoğanist paramilitary in Turkey*

* The initial version of this chapter first appeared as an article on the PPJ website on 30.5.2018.

> *Government is an institution which prevents injustice
> other than such as it commits itself.*
>
> Ibn Khaldun (1332 – 1406 AD)

ERDOĞAN'S NOVELTY: SETTING THE REPRESSION

IT IS BEYOND DOUBT THAT AN AUTOCRAT SHOULD HAVE A variety of tactics to keep his time-horizon as wid as possible. In one hand, he should allow elections so as to create a democratic façade and thus enhancing the regime's legitimacy, in other words, he should develop some kind of "emergency preparedness toolkit" against worst case scenarios with a particular potential of overthrowing.

Although pieces of evidence within the last decade demonstrated the extent to which the Erdoğanist roots derived from the apparatuses of the Turkish-style "Deep State" largely represented by the twin precedents, JİTEM (controversial Gendarmerie Intelligence Organisation) and Ultranationalists, his model offers some true novelty.

Firstly, novelty is especially true as regards to the size and nature of the "coalition" put against dissents, and Islamist ideology within which the process is camouflaged. In that coalition-making process, as an Islamist leader – who uses and abuses Islam as a cover for his dictatorship – Erdoğan naturalised the connection commonly made between Islam, the state as a secular power, and violence. Indeed, he achieved to form alliances across the secular and religious divide, shifting boundaries and combining Islamist ideology with a nationalist narrative.

Islamism has a particular importance as a tool enhanced by Erdoğan and his intellectual advisors, being in the office as a "system" based upon the exploitation of religious sentiments – a system that tends to distort the original message of religion and that has an inherent tendency to generate crises.

This system is very coherent with Erdoğan's effort to intimidate the Gülen sympathisers by attaching a religious meaning to alleged sufferings that "patriotic" citizens experienced in struggle with the coup plotters. However, Erdoğan has found less Gülenists fallen while his efforts have often turned into a kind of *exorcism,* where he, through the use of violence, was trying to remove the evil Gülen sympathisers from the Turkish social body.

Secondly, the pro-Erdoğan coalition differs from the previous social engineering projects of Turkey both in size and victimisation patterns adopted with the following reasons.

Subsequent to the July 15 coup attempt, under the autocracy of Erdoğan, different – even contesting in some extent – players of the political theatre i. e. the legislative, judiciary, and executive branches of the State, the ruling party and its right-wing alliances, army, police, intelligence, leading gang and mafia groups, celebrities, religious establishment, mainstream media, academia, trade unions, and business oligarchy have altogether positioned themselves against one single enemy: the Gülen Movement. From the Islamist vantage, those people qualified as "heretics" worthy of being exterminated.

This progress made Erdoğan himself the only one who benefits from the coup attempt while pushing the Gülen Movement further into the margins of the society. From the perspective of T. Khalil (2016) studying on dissenting people put at the target of the state in South Asia, they have thus become "*homo sacers* (accursed men) – men and women who are no longer covered by legal, civil and political rights; men and women who cease being citizens and become bare lives; men and women who can be abducted; men and women who can be held *incommunicado* in secret detention facilities; men and women who can be tortured to death."[1] *(See figure 10, page 224)*

Thus, the interests of this "oversized" coalition ultimately became essentially a joint enterprise that may later give birth to a violent repression – if not civil war – through off-the-book operations.

In this article, with reference to some major steps that have been taken towards oppression and covert operations, we will attempt to explore three key items packed into the Erdoğanist toolkit, by the effects they may produce:

1. *paramilitary death squads derived either from the instability of Syria or pro-AKP youth clubs (seedbed effect),*

2. *a primary service provider to equip them with necessary skills like cold-blooded execution (SADAT-type effect), and,*

3. *legal immunity for those who are killing in the name of the Erdoğan regime (impunity effect).*

Assuming that an autocrat does not risk losing the election

---

1. G. Agamben (1998) from whom Khalil borrowed the term, with reference to archaic Roman law, describes *Homo Sacer* as "the one whom the people have judged on account of a crime. It is not permitted to sacrifice this man, yet he who kills him will not be condemned for homicide" (see chapter 4).

and instead uses any means to guarantee continuation of his regime is the point of departure for this article which also seeks to identify some significant aspects of his "preparedness."

"TRAIN-AND-EQUIP" PROGRAM FOR THE JIHADIST FIGHTERS: FOR WHAT?

During the 2010 s, Erdoğan of Turkey undertook a series of constitutional/political changes that gave him personal control over the executive and judiciary branches and reshaped the country as an aggressive power in the Middle East. The latter was accompanied by a foreign policy based on a *neo-Ottomanist* narrative that is associated with the u. s. neo-imperialism. Today, is that enough to satisfy Erdoğan?

It is fair to answer: no, never. So, no emergency kit is complete without a paramilitary force with an absolute loyalty not to the State, but to the ruler at the top. Given the traditionally "defensive" structure of the Army, and Police prevailing with the "law enforcement" function, he needs some ancillary force in order to maintain one-man-rule at home.

On 21.2.2015, news agencies announced an agreement[2] signed between the u. s. and Turkey aiming at training and equipping the "moderate" Syrian militias against the Assad regime. Whether the militias are really moderate is another question and is being highly debated in other medias (for example, see the article by Patrick Cockburn[3] which appeared on the *Counterpunch*). As B. Turbeville (2015) put it, since at least 2010 both countries have been complicit in the arming, funding,

---

2. http: //www. bbc. com/news/world-middle-east-31 511 376 (Accessed: 25 May 2018).
3. https://www.counterpunch.org/2018/02/12/is-turkey-recruiting-ex-isis-fighters/ (Accessed: 25 May 2018).

directing, training, and facilitating of terrorist death squads in Syria. And that was fully compliant with Erdoğan's long-run political agenda.

Since then, Turkey has hosted a number of terrorist groups that, in appearance, have been at the forefront of the war against Damascus. The military operations *Euphrates Shield* and *Olive Branch* were fresh cases in which they had an opportunity to display the degree of their brutality and repression. Both operations also acknowledged that, as well as being a landing spot for many ISIL militants fleeing Syria, Turkey has turned into the crucible of jihadist mobilizastion. *(See figure 11, page 225)*

Nevertheless, many tend to assume Turkey employs these militants for special operations in Syria against Assad and/or Kurdish rebels. If such is the case, this leads us to the following question: In a country where almost 70 % of the citizens live in debt,[4] namely near the edge of subsistence, and where 10.6 % are jobless (19 % young persons) in the last quarter of 2018 according to the official statistics,[5] why does a regime devote its limited resources to such a heavy-cost and risky program?

A report from the *Institute for Economics and Peace*, The Economic Value of Peace – 2016,[6] showed that the economic impact of violence and conflict for Turkey, in purchasing power parity (PPP) terms, was about $129 billion in 2015. This is equivalent to 9.7 % of GDP or $1.700 PPP per annum, per person. Report ranks Turkey 50th out of 163 countries. It is also worthy of note that the expenditure occurred in responding to the refugee inflows since the start of the Syrian crisis (about $30 billion as

---

4. http://www.tuik.gov.tr/PreHaberBultenleri.do?id=24 579 (Accessed: 25 May 2018).
5. http://www.tuik.gov.tr/HbGetirHTML.do?id=27 688 (Accessed: 25 May 2018).
6. http://economicsandpeace.org/wp-content/uploads/2016/12/The-Economic-Value-of-Peace-2016-WEB.pdf (Accessed: 25 May 2018).

of 2017, a Parliamentary Report mentions[7]) is not counted in the report.

Against this, from the Annual Activity Report – 2016 of the [former] Ministry of Family and Social Policies,[8] we learn what has been done for the victims of violence and conflict (martyrs, veterans, and their relatives in legal sense):

1. *country-wide religious memorial services (mevlit) at mosques,*

2. *500.000 packs of candy gifts (mevlit şekeri) handed out to participants, and*

3. *a total of 5.079 ministerial condolence letters sent to the martyrs' mothers.*

Great! No word on the compensation or financial redress. A very impressive response that only suits an Islamist regime.

Before this miserable picture, we should also be asking: for which purpose is governmental capacity being assigned to build extra-legal entities at the cost of putting citizens' security at risk, as well as being recognized as a "gang-state" engaging in acts of aggression against its neighbours?

Maybe to facilitate the overthrow of the Assad regime: as increasing evidence showed, rather than particular interventions of countries like Turkey, this partly depends on the cohesion of involving figures and interactions between the global powers. Or maybe, to ensure border security: this requires

---

7. https://www.tbmm.gov.tr/komisyon/insanhaklari/docs/2018/goc_ve_uyum_raporu.pdf (Accessed: 25 May 2018).
8. Annual Activity Report-2016: https://sgb.aile.gov.tr/uploads/pages/arge-raporlar/2016-yili-faaliyet-raporu.pdf (Accessed: 5 August 2018).

adopting the opposite policy i. e. taking measures mitigating the permeability of the borderline.

Such naïve answers therefore remain like attempts to square the circle. There should be another explanation to invest in violence and conflict through **death squads**.

From the **political** perspective, Campbell (2002) links the appearance of death squads to a crisis of the modern state and considers them as one instance of a much wider process of "subcontracting" that characterizes nearly all states in the twentieth century. Emergence of death squads therefore signals a deep crisis within the state. So, they differ from other tools of repression in a number of significant aspects, notably in the way they mix state and private interests and in the way they call into question the legitimacy of the state.

As far as the **organisational** aspect is concerned, we have first seen these jihadist groups taking part in the cross-border operations alongside the Army units. It is very clear that they are formed as entities having their own hierarchies and they are not part of Turkish military organogram. Paramilitary activities have to be autonomous of the armed forces, because "plausible deniability" is critical to the military if it wanted to preserve the image of legitimacy necessary to secure both foreign and domestic trust. Connections with the state agents like military, police, and intelligence, however, should remain unofficial for strategic and tactical reasons (Mazzei, 2009).

Apart from the hierarchical autonomy, new-born jihadist fighters [Erdoğan and his surrogates in media call them all "Free Syrian Army" which is indeed a kind of umbrella gathering wide range of *Salafi-jihadi* groups including ISIL and Al-Nusra] essentially differ from the "provisional village guards" whose tasks and responsibilities are described by Law no. 442 on the village administrations⁹ [N. B. : as of 3 October 2016, article 8 of the Decree Law no. 676 replaced the term provisional village guard with the "security guard"; they are no longer "provisional"]. Since there is no legal framework to apply, jihadist groups deserve to be described as *extra-legal* organisations.

Furthermore, they do not display a homogenous category in *nationality* terms. They are being gathered not only from among Syrian origin people but also from a wide range of nationalities in Central Asia and Europe including Azerbaijan, Russia (Chechnya), Tajikistan, Kazakhstan, China (Uighur Turks) and of course Turkey. No common sense of national self exists to take place in a national rebel.

Then, the most obvious question, of course, is who is to rule? Who gathers these less-homogenous fighters under the same pattern of operation?

What feature distinguishes them is being affiliated with Erdoğan through the MİT. What we have seen, however, is a kind of paramilitary unit designed for JİTEM-style[10] covert operations going beyond empowerment of traditional security forces. From some incident they caused in Syria, we can more or less grasp their *modus operandi:* operate like a death squad, a mass killing machine. Incidents also revealed that there is no regular control by the Army personnel to ensure a bit of discipline; they do not work under the direct control of the military chain of command.

It would therefore be a great delusion to see them as some *ad hoc* formation which will expire when the Syrian crises ended. It is well known that once any organisation is established, it will in time elude the tasks declared and tend to an existence

---

9. Law no. 442 was published in the Official Gazette of 7 April 1924, with no. 68.
10. For some details of JİTEM operations, see: https://kurdistancommentary.wordpress.com/2009/02/09/jitem-deep-state/(Accessed: 25 May 2018).

for its sake and for its fruits. Turkish readers may recall how the "provisional" village guards recruited from among Kurdish tribesmen to "protect" villages against the PKK gradually turned into local paramilitary forces stealing, killing, kidnapping and raping with impunity.

On the other hand, in **legal** terms, the Turkey-U. S. agreement concerning the Train-and-Equip Program has not been submitted to the Parliament; neither was it published as an annex to a Cabinet decree. However, we know, in September 2014, the U. S. Congress[11] authorized the Train-and-Equip program for "moderate opposition forces in Syria as one of several lines of effort to fight the Islamic State of Iraq and the Levant (ISIL)" with a budget of $500 million.

We also know from the Statement dated 9 October 2015 implying the failure of the strategy –to pull fighters out of Syria, teach them advanced combat skills and return them to face the ISIL – the Pentagon, after only thirteen months, abandoned the program and instead directed its efforts to provision of equipment packages and weapons to the selected rebel groups on the ground.[12] However, as understood from the recent operations, the Erdoğan regime still continues to work with the jihadist fighters, bringing them to Turkey for training before infiltrating them into Syria.

Seen from the **financial** angle, corresponding costs for Turkey encompass not only training and equipping expenditures but also accommodation, subsistence, healthcare, and occasional transfer services to be covered by the hosting coun-

---

11. http://www.fas.org/sgp/crs/natsec/R43 727.pdf (Accessed: 25 May 2018).
12. https://www.defense.gov/News/News-Releases/News-Release-View/Article/622 610/statement-on-syria/(Accessed: 25 May 2018).

try.[13] This also requires specific budgetary arrangements or covert financial transfers. However, despite more than three years passed, concerning the total cost of the Train-and-Equip program, neither spokesmen of the Erdoğanist regime have shared any figure with the public nor was this matter discussed in the media and parliament.

Who will pay the bill? Who are the principal financiers or sponsors for this big-ticket program? Qatar or Saudis, or both? No exact official response has been received so far. What we know is that all the costs are ultimately to be paid by the taxpayers even though such seems to cause no concern on their side at the moment.

From an **economy-political** perspective, escalating the level of repressive violence, to some extent, may be a reasonable choice to prolong the lifetime in the office. As Mason and Crane (1989) suggested, that is certainly the case when marginal economic security of non-elite households (commoners) was eroded by economic and demographic transformations that accompany dependent modes of development. Such a shaky economy renders them more vulnerable to subsistence crises and therefore more susceptible to opposition parties.

At this point, violence and mass terror directed against opposition may reduce voters' willingness to engage in support of the opposition. Although they hold some criticisms of the ruling party, they feel that the alternative to the ruling party was

---

13. On 27 July 2018, Khaled al-Khateb from Al-Monitor reported that the families of "Free Syrian Army" fighters who died in the operation Olive Branch have obtained death gratuity payments from the Turkish government in June. Each bereaved family obtained 60.000 Turkish liras (about $12.500 at that time) in addition to ongoing monthly payments of $100. It was also reported that other benefits such as being granted Turkish citizenship are still being examined on the Turkish side. Furthermore, on 12 8. 2018, Reuters, with reference to an interview with the commander of the "National Army", a jihadist group backed by Turkey of Erdoğan, reported that "Turkish support includes fighters' wages, logistical support and weapons if necessary."

chaos or violence. They value stability over democratization. Such an *ad hoc* violence, however, rather than by police and/or army with their classical organisation, can be best achieved in practice through death squads specialised in terror.

For the pro-Erdoğan front, the experiments right after the general elections of 7 June 2015 in which the AKP failed to take the office alone proved that the masses can eventually be terrorized into compliance. The experiments with vehicle-suicide bombings also showed how violence contributes to the overthrow of civil society and to herding ordinary people.

The main lesson learned from this process which ended on 2 November of 2015, a date of – constitutionally mandatory – election on which the AKP regained the office was, however, the necessity of sorting out the conditions under which violence deters or, alternatively, stimulates voter support for the opposition.

So, as repression and violence become more pervasive and more arbitrary, its deterrent effect on the support of the opposition should diminish because the likelihood of becoming a victim is no longer related to one's support or non-support of dissents (Mason & Crane, 1989). That was the case in the Southeast Turkey where security services brutally crushed mostly unarmed civilian Kurdish population throughout the years of 2016 – 17. Therefore opposition grew up with new siders and thus remained prevalent in that part of the country.

From the **psycho-sociological** point of view, the systematic disenfranchisement of certain parts of the population, if it is conducted by security forces through curfews, arbitrary jailing etc. , may be a trigger of social upheaval.

Dissociation, traumatization or victimization may also play a key role in motivating individuals to join armed groups as a way of actively dealing with their trauma and negative feelings of victimization (Ferguson & Burgess, 2009). If no one from the Gülen sympathisers community took up arms regardless of the brutality and oppression they collectively faced after the failed coup of 15 July, this is obviously an exception that needs to be a subject of scientific research.

Autocrat, in any case, taking the "deniability" notion of Campbell (2002) into consideration, should value private death squads over terrorism by the public security forces [for deniability, see the below section].

At present [May 2018], under the shadow of the upcoming snap election of **24 June** which is both Presidential and Parliamentary, the overwhelming fear at the pro-Erdoğan camp is that the head of political office would change (be it through elections or arms) and would investigate the theft and confiscations of property involved by the Erdoğanist oligarchy.

Once such a fear occupies the minds at the top, repression and violence substitute for the rule of law. As the samples from the political history showed, when they felt short time-horizons, autocrats become capable of turning to their nastiest levels of repression, and ultimately mass killings. Besides other factors, a looming **economic crisis** may narrow this horizon. It is in such an atmosphere that paramilitary death squad activities tend to flourish.

Optimistic voters may have pleasure with the "hot money" that has been transferred from the Gulf. The truth however gives no pleasure indeed: A recent study by *Global Financial Integrity*[14] found that the total "illicit financial flow" that entered Turkey from outside in 2014 accounts for 13 % of the total trade size, $399.787 million. No problem at first glance.

---

14. http://www.gfintegrity.org/wp-content/uploads/2017/05/GFI-IFF-Report-2017_final.pdf (Accessed: 25 May 2018).

Bear in mind that, in countries like Turkey with a hegemonic ruling party, huge amounts of illicit financial inflows are allowed only to serve the greedy rulers at the top and somehow elude national accounting and taxation procedures. Such volatile short-term inflows give nothing to economy other than short-run recovery in its balance of the current account. Therefore, this percentage, in a large extent, represents total social-economic costs falling on tax payers.

Erdoğan, through his surrogates in the media, evaluated the time between 7 June and 2 November 2015 creating a self-fulfilling narrative that the country is under the danger of becoming divided. As could be recalled, this narrative was being accompanied by bombing-suicide attacks with indiscriminative character, and praise of "martyrdom" that makes the tragedy of violence more acceptable to some degree.

But, for today and near future, to strengthen the "Presidential system," Erdoğan needs to direct the scope to internal and external enemies which he already listed as pro-PKK Kurds, leftists, Gülen sympathisers, Israel, and Western forces. For enemies inside, it is the paramilitary death squads to which this *strategy* suits best. Those who seek peace can only be repressed with this means.

In brief, thanks to the instability in Syria, in addition to the existing armed units i. e. (1) the Army including the Gendarmerie, (2) the Police – in a highly militarised form, and (3) the South-eastern Security Guards, Erdoğan has added the last wagon to the long train of repressive violence in Turkey: (4) SADAT – trained death squads mainly planted in the soil of Syria.

SADAT: PRECURSOR TO THE ERDOĞANIST DEATH SQUADS

The police and army, being under the governmental authority, also because of the nature of their capabilities and responsibilities, are restricted, to some extent, to operate as primary counter-insurgency forces in all countries and remain as law enforcement bodies. This restriction ultimately leads autocrats to invoke some **patriotic formations** like mercenary terrorists, vigilante groups, or death squads without the constraints of being a government entity.

In a broader sense, death squads can be defined as "pro-government groups who engage in extrajudicial killings of people they define as enemies of the state, whose members are, either directly or indirectly, connected with the government and/or security forces. There is usually overlap in membership and various forms of collusion –including the provision of weapons and intelligence – between the death squads and the security forces" (Sluka, 2000b).

The death squad phenomenon is not unique to Turkey, but takes its roots from the post-colonial world: ORDEN (Organización Democrática Nacionalista) in El Salvador (1970 – 80 s), *Grupo Colina* of Peru during Fujimori (1990 – 2000), the French-supported *Red Hand* against Algerian nationalists, and *Operation Black Eye* against Viet Cong are well known samples. They were responsible for countless assassinations and disappearances through 1960 s to 1980 s across the globe.

From the overall findings in the literature, it seems safe to conclude that, initially, many of the death squads were inspired by the organisation set up following the CIA-inspired overthrow of pro-Marxist governments in Latin America. The suppression of Communist insurgency was one of the most significant factors leading to these extra-legal formations. By the time, various kinds of opposition movements (ethnic or religious minorities in Africa and Southeast Asia) were included into the menu.

Such arguments answer the question of why and how death squads emerge. Major factor for the use of death squads, however, lies in the need of states to deny that they are breaking established norms of behaviour. The modern state is bound by a whole range of internal and external norms that place strict limits on a state's range of options –if respected. Only death squads and other covert means provide plausible deniability of state involvement in violent acts (Campbell, 2002).

When death squads or vigilante groups undertake political terror for the state, that is to root out political opposition to the state, they also express the inadequacy of the power of the state, albeit frustration with the cumbersome nature of legitimate forms of authority, power, and coercion (Couto, 2010).

Another finding also becomes crystal clear in the literature: Turkey of Erdoğan is not alone on the planet. As anthropologist J. Sluka (2000 a) argued, individual states that engaged in campaigns of state terror are part of an "international structure" or network since state terror is a global phenomenon and local cases are only comprehensible within this encapsulating context.

Having organised under the auspices of the MİT, SADAT Inc. or "International Defence Consultancy" ("SADAT *Uluslararası Savunma Danışmanlık İnşaat Sanayi ve Ticaret* A. Ş." in Turkish) apparently is not included into the national budget, nor were there any laws, regulations, hearings, or official meetings leaving a paper trail detailing its creation.

However, at first sight, SADAT does not appear as a dark organisation of the Erdoğan regime, nor is it a death squad or paramilitary force for Erdoğan, but a private company, of which the Corporation Charter was published in the Journal of Turkish Trade Registry on 28 2. 2012. SADAT, in actual sense, has been functioning with a notary approved contract since 22 2. 2011.

By the way, a report by the Sound of Silence Group (SoS, 2017) draws attention to the meaning of "SADAT" which is not an acronym: in Arabic, it is the plural form of the word *Seyyid* which literally means "the Big Boss, Patron, Grand, and Chief". Majuscules are to evoke this bigness. [Turkish readers may recall the phrase "Sadat-ı Kiram" that refers to honourable big men in the *Sufi* orders[15]]. Then, who is the Big Boss? SADAT is directly tied to Erdoğan from scratch, though it operated and evolved in more of a quasi-state fashion.

We learn from the Corporation Charter that SADAT, under the chairmanship of Adnan Tanrıverdi, a – cashiered – brigadier general, Chief Military Advisor to Erdoğan since August 2016, was established in İstanbul with a capital of 643.000 TL [this amount was marked up to 880.000 TL on 15 July 2016, with a further 30 shareholders] by 23 Turkish citizens most of whom retired soldiers with various ranks.

In turkish conditions, this amount of capital can be considered normal for companies with advisory and training capability. As can be seen below, relevant facilities, logistical arrangements, and equipment necessary for trainings promised, however, dwarfs the capital concerned.

64 retired soldiers who served within the military network, as well as being known to have close affiliations with the AKP are also recruited as military experts or advisors. Training and expertise fields can be seen on the SADAT website: http: //www. sadat. com.tr/tr/

Both shareholders and other staff are more likely to be loyal

---

15. See, for example: https://sorularlaislamiyet.com/sadat-i-kiram-ne-demektir-0 (Accessed: 25 May 2018).

to the state and have presumably received relevant training to some degree, with a trainer capacity as well. At first, their track record under the official chain of command clearly links SADAT to the state agents.

Seen from this angle, SADAT cannot simply be considered as a private entity competing in the market, but rather the one designed to serve as the structural and conceptual precursor for Erdoğan's paramilitary groups linked with the state by their decisiveness to stop whatever potential success the opposition might have. The following instance may give an insight into the position SADAT occupies at the top of the state.

Concerning the operation Olive Branch in Afrin of Syria, a security summit[16] chaired by Erdoğan was held on 23 1. 2018. The founder of SADAT, Adnan Tanrıverdi (most likely with the title of the security advisor), alongside the PM, Chief of General Staff, deputy prime ministers and head of MİT, attended the meeting.[17]

From the Trade Registry of 26 8. 2016, right after the abortive coup of 15 July, we learn that he left the chief executive position but remained among the members of the executive board. On the same date, his son, Ali Kamil Melih Tanrıverdi, was elected as the Chief Executive of SADAT. His writings in the *BlogSpot*[18] affirm that the son resembles his father: Ali Kamil is also sympathetic to extremist Islamist ideologies.

On its website, SADAT declares its purpose as "assisting in the self-sufficient military force of the world of Islam" by serving in the fields of military training and maintenance. As SoS

---

16. https://news.sol.org.tr/turkish-governments-paramilitary (Accessed: 26 May 2018).
17. Tanrıverdi was subsequently appointed to the membership of the Palatial "Board of Security and Foreign Policy" by the Presidential Decision no. 2018/196 of 9 October 2018.
18. http://akmtanriverdi.blogspot.com.tr/2014/07/isidin-misyonu.html (Accessed: 26 May 2018).

(2017) rightly identified, this makes the Erdoğan regime SADAT's prominent client, who is ultimately interested in advancing his own benefits under the mask of helping Muslim populations and countries. Then, how works SADAT to this end?

SADAT, from its website, offers a detailed list of training with a particular emphasis on the unconventional warfare, i. e. psychological warfare and operations, ambush, sabotage, raid, destruction, road closing, assassination, rescue and abduction, terror, type of street actions, and operation techniques consisting of secret activities as well as courses on aviation and individual combat trainings. Yet we could not find any price list for the trainings SADAT provides.

During the course of trainings, SADAT trainers, in addition to training facilities or camps necessary by the nature, normally would be in need of using numerous high-price tools and equipment such as weapons, bombs, ammunitions, helicopters, aircrafts, speedboat, electronic simulation kit, naval mines, land and water vehicles, night vision devices, and intelligence, surveillance, and reconnaissance (ISR) equipment, among other items. Most of them can only be found in the inventory of the Army, and of the Police to some extent, and – in legal terms – they need to be "registered."

Furthermore, whether military or not, no private actor in Turkey is allowed to import, install, operate, and use these equipment legally. However, on its website, SADAT still refers to the legislations such as Law no. 5202[19] on "the Safety of Defence Industry," Law no. 5201[20] on "the Supervision of Industrial Facilities Producing Combat Vehicles and Equipment, Weapon, Ammunition and Explosives," and other secondary regulations.

---

19. http://www.msb.gov. tr/Content/Upload/Docs/teknikhizmetler/EK-B_5202_Sayili_Kanun.doc (Accessed: 25 May 2018).
20. http://www.msb.gov.tr/Content/Upload/Docs/teknikhizmetler/EK-A%205 201%20 Say%C4%B1l%C4%B1%20Kanun.doc (Accessed: 25 May 2018).

SADAT however, within its denunciation of 16 8. 2017[21] to the prosecutor concerning some allegations[22] raised by a news platform, still introduces itself as a company operating in line with the provisions of the above-mentioned laws which are totally irrelevant to what it does.

In brief, the legal framework concerning the defence industry does not leave any room to SADAT-type "service" companies in the defence sector. That is to say, not service providers but suppliers can operate in the sector under the supervision of the Ministry of National Defence (MoD). Furthermore, a lack of a legal framework for any sector does not necessarily imply that this sector is open to private actors. In Turkey, normal people are not allowed to purchase a combat helicopter for example. It is illegal to organise trainings with military or paramilitary character as well.

SADAT's illegality is also revealed by its correspondences with the MoD on the scope of the Turkish defence industry. According to its informative booklet, SADAT *Gerçeği* (SADAT Reality),[23] SADAT submitted a document concerning the supervision of defence consultancy and military training services to the MoD in 2012. However, the MoD, in its response, underlined that the defence industry service sector is not covered by any legislation in Turkey and that they had no supervision task in this respect.

Further to this attempt, SADAT requested that the defence industry "service" sector be included into the above mentioned laws, by submitting a draft law to several ministries in 2013, but received no response.

---

21. http://www.sadat.com.tr/tr/haberler/haberler/351-parlamento-haber-sitesi-hakkinda-suc-duyurusu-ve-tekzip.html (Accessed: 25 May 2018).
22. https://www.parlamentohaber.com/iste-yeni-kontrgerilla/(Accessed: 25 May 2018).
23. http://www.sadat.com.tr/tr/haberler/haberler/357-sadat-gercegi.htm (Accessed: 25 May 2018).

All these constraints necessarily lead SADAT, through protection by Erdoğan, to be linked with the Army and/or Intelligence services. It is therefore a natural necessity for such a company to use the Army-owned weapons and facilities in its "commercial" activities. As evidence, some media reported that, in addition to training camps[24] in Kırşehir, Hatay (Apaydın, adjacent to Syrian refugee camp), and Tokat provinces, the Turkish Naval Forces' Ulaşlı training camp in Gölcük (Kocaeli) was in use of SADAT for a while.

It has been reported by many observers[25] that training, logistics, and transfer affairs of the jihadist fighters gathered from the different countries listed above were being organised by SADAT while Turkish consulates in Russia evidently provide Turkish passports for the fighters from the Caucasus region.

Several media reports, for example SoS (2017), also argue that SADAT-trained death squads were responsible for many civilian killings during the coup attempt of 15 July, including the brutal killings of cadets and conscripts who had already surrendered to the police. However, the prosecutor has not initiated any procedure to investigate the allegations concerning lynching, killings, and beheadings while many murders and disappearances still remained undiscovered.

Although SADAT utterly rejects these allegations, activities foreseen to be realised and provisions within its Charter refutes its denial:[26] On its website, SADAT, with a haughty tone, declares a mission of "establishing the cooperation among the Islamic countries in the sense of military and defence industries […]."

---

24. http://www.abcgazetesi.com/abc-yasadisi-silahli-egitim-kamplarini-belgeledi-yedi-kamptan-biri-de-istanbulda-74 831 h.htm (Accessed: 25 May 2018).
25. http://www.aei.org/publication/has-sadat-become-Erdoğans-revolutionary-guards/ (Accessed: 25 May 2018).
26. http://www.sadat.com.tr/tr/haberler/haberler/357-sadat-gercegi.htm (Accessed: 25 May 2018).

In accordance with this mission, the SADAT website contains some naïve scenarios written by Adnan Tanrıverdi, for example a 20-day war to defeat Israel through donations by each Islamic country to Palestine: one submarine, one war plane, one tank etc. This is followed by some Islamist narratives concerning the alleged potential of the Islamic world on the one hand, describing the Western states as "imperialist", "crusader" countries on the other.

Furthermore, article 3 of the Charter describes the aim and subject of SADAT as

1. *"taking the interest of the Republic of Turkey, to provide defence consultancy, organisation, and training of the friendly countries in need, and provisioning weapons, ammunition, device-equipment, food and livery for them (sub-para. 3.1),*

2. *to create a climate of cooperation for defence and the defence industry among friendly countries, [...] marketing for the products of Turkish defence industry, [...] to provide inter-state organisations on the relevant matters (sub-para. 3.2),*

3. *to build and operate sporting, training, firing and simulation systems and facilities concerning personnel, vehicle, ship, plane, helicopter, material, and weapons that may be needed by a security force, and to provide practical trainings therein (sub-para. 3.5)*

It is obvious that, apart from being highly nationalist and pro-state, from a political point of view, such objectives can only be expressed at government-level. Probably because of this reason, one year later from its establishment, on 28 2. 2012, the first two sub-paragraphs were amended but the mission remained unchanged.

On the opposite side, whether SADAT is doing wrong things has been a matter of concern since the founding of the company. As an example, SoS (2017) assertively argues;

> *On 15th July 2016, SADAT immediately mobilized pro-Erdoğan paramilitary groups as soon as the tanks started to roll in the streets at the beginning of the self-coup. These groups comprised paramilitary forces like "Ottoman Hearths" [Osmanlı Ocakları] whose members received unconventional warfare tactics from SADAT against formal troops [...]. For countervailing against the revolting factions of the regular army, SADAT played a crucial role in favour of Erdoğan's rule through its own operatives as well as the Ak Youth militias [...].*

It was also argued that SADAT is affiliated with the jihadist organisations al-Qaida, al-Nusra, and ISIL while Eissenstat (2017) argues that it is also providing protection to the Erdoğan regime inside Turkey.

Against these allegations, SADAT, in the SADAT *Gerçeği*, claims that they have not provided any training services to any country or group, nor do they operate any training facility. If such is the case, it must be a kind of charity organisation!

Without further assessment of the mentioned allegations flying around this organisation, it is very clear from its charter that the primary purpose of SADAT is to provide training on certain unconventional warfare topics. SADAT, on the other hand, seems to become a central element in Erdoğan's survival strategy targeting dissents. We can therefore link the hard-edged, violent, paramilitary image of SADAT to his long-run political agenda. This linkage is especially the norm in particular moments security forces could not operate overtly on the ground.

As for the **pro-Erdoğan youth organisations** like Ottoman Hearths, originally, such clubs often serve to build strong party ties at the neighbourhood level and as a source of patronage for party loyalists (Eissenstat, 2017). Initially, these pro-Erdoğan clubs were devised as pivotal civilian forces to suppress dissidents during anti-Erdoğan protests. That was the case in the *Gezi Park* protests in June 2013 where they caught public attention for the first time. The motivation behind it was also the same when they assaulted the pro-Kurdish HDP (People's Democratic Party) buildings and some media outlets.

From this point of view, these organisations are not actually paramilitary but rather gatherings mobilised through social hatred which Erdoğan's forceful personality and intolerant stance against the opposition incited. This is very compliant with the patriarchal social order motivating males in *macho cultures* that praise honour and courage. The Erdoğan regime's novelty is to combine this macho culture with a highly dosed *Islamist* ideology that turns its followers to dogmatists to eliminate all opponents in Turkey.

Nonetheless, we can maintain, it makes sense to see them as gatherings for generating a repertoire of possible ways of repression: (1) as Çubukçu (2018) puts it, "inflicting fear among citizens and to oppress political dissidents by granting immunity for the youths' criminal offenses against Erdoğan's political enemies", and (2) functioning as a "seedbed" in which the brightest ones are transplanted by SADAT-type organisations for paramilitary purposes.

The latter is strongly related to the following: the post-15 July Erdoğanist security initiative wants to cherry-pick individuals from scratch and secretly place them in paramilitary groups even while they maintained contacts with the National Intelligence, the MİT, and security agencies including underground Deep State organisations. The interactions between SADAT and would-be-candidates from Syrian jihadists and pro-AKP youth organisations are characterised by this new initiative which is built out of a recognition that military and police services are incapable of confronting the issues raised by Erdoğan's war on dissents.

On the other hand, such security initiatives are not unique to Turkey and in fact – more or less – resemble those of some Muslim countries. For example, in 1971, to repress the insurrection in East Pakistan (today's Bangladesh), West Pakistani generals decided to raise a special counter-insurgency unit, *Al-Badr* [an allusion to the Battle of Badr, the first war fought by the Prophet Muhammad and his followers]. Its members were pro-Pakistan Bengalis, recruited from the ranks of Islamist groups like *Jamaat-el-Islami* and its student wing. They were trained to undertake "specialised operations" – abducting, torturing and executing political opponents, especially Bengali intellectuals (Khalil, 2016).

This was also true for Indonesia in 1965 where members of *Ansor* [derived from the term *Ansar* in Arabic, "the Helpers" that refers to Muslim Madinan inhabitants who sheltered Prophet Muhammad and his companions, *Mohajirin*], the youth organisation of the Islamist party, *Nahdat-ul-Ulama* (the Awakening of Muslim Scholars), helped the army forces in mass killings of alleged "Communist" and front group members, and suspected sympathisers (van der Kroef, 1987).

To this, prior to the 1965 coup attempt, Ansor had founded

a paramilitary unit, "Banser," in preparation for confrontations with the PKI *(Communist Party of Indonesia)*. Even in January 1966, the NU leadership endorsed the *"Guidebook for Indoctrination to Eliminate the Thinking of PKI/Gestapu"* in which the editor claimed it was a form of worship (*ibadah*) to crush the PKI and that "the PKI must be wiped out from the face of Indonesia and never given the chance to exist again." *The second largest Islamist organisation of the country, Muhammadiyah, also provided rapid support for crushing the PKI, with some leaders declaring this a religious duty (McGregor, 2009).*

From the angle of international relations, as R. Yellinek (2018) highlighted, these interactions may also create a real danger to the European countries: "the fact that Erdoğan operates a private militia means that he can do everything he wants without the limitations and reviews from the other government arms." However, today this seems to cause less concern in their part.

LEGISLATE-TO-KILL: IMMUNITY BY THE "BLACK LAWS"

Both paramilitary and security forces that engage in extra-judicial killings and disappearances, as well as torture of actual or suspected members of the terrorist organisation or their sympathisers need to be immune from prosecution and other legal proceedings. So their operations may sometimes include indiscriminate bombings of villages, random arrests of men, torture and killing of the detained, murders by death squadrons, stealing and destroying the property of the local residents including arson attacks on their houses, and rape of both men and women.

Codifying such immunity into law is therefore vital for

the deployment of death squads across the country as well as applying lethal forms of violence with impunity. In other words, "legislate-to-kill" precedes "shoot-to-kill". Needless to say, that is in strong contrast to **the right to life** described under article 2 of the ECHR imposing a general duty to protect peopleslives.

The Erdoğan regime, however, through legislation mechanisms, clearly turned Turkey into a country where lives are put at specific risk by state action or inaction. Under the dust of the on-going killings and destruction of cities across the Kurdish populated provinces in Southern Anatolia, Erdoğan, on 14 July of 2016, just one day before the abortive coup, promulgated Law no. 6722 that granted the military personnel and government officials blanket immunity from prosecution and other legal proceedings for "any casualty, damage to life and property, violation of rights, physical or mental damage" during the counter-insurgency operations.[27]

Article 12 of Law no. 6722, adding a new paragraph to article 11 of Law no. 5442 concerning provincial governance, empowers the Cabinet, when the capability of the general law enforcement bodies, i. e. police and gendarmerie, remains insufficient to repress an upheaval or serious threat to public order, to assign the Turkish Armed Forces to the war on terror under the coordination of the governors.

The article also reads that, in their operations, Turkish Armed Forces can do "searches without warrant in houses and offices." That is legally considered within the scope of the military service and duties and the courts cannot issue any order to seize, detain or arrest those who committed criminal acts. Damages are being paid by the government as well. The claim for damages caused by breaches driven by decisions, transactions, and activities by both military and civil personnel can

---

27. Law no. 6722 was published in the Official Gazette of 14 July 2016, with no. 29 770.

only be directed to the state. That is the norm even for individual breaches like offense, torture, rape, murder or other actions.

Under these circumstances, if deemed necessary, initiating a prosecution process is subject to the approval of the local or central superiors identified within the article. These immunities are also applicable to the security guards and voluntary security guards numbering 50.793 and 19.993 gunmen respectively.[28]

The article in question was indeed designed to terrorise the population and shield agents of the state from censure or prosecution for abuses. Such provisions are also *de facto* licences for torture, murder, enforced disappearance, and other forms of violence. As such, it seems to be a deliberate part of the whole scenario involving the abortive coup and subsequent crackdowns.

Whether enacted by parliament (law) or by the cabinet (decree law), if any law ensures that "no suit, prosecution or other legal proceedings shall be against any member of the army, police, and other security apparatuses for anything which is done or intended to be done in any operation," it is a **Black Law**.

The term black law was first used by Mohandas Gandhi to describe some British colonial laws legitimising preventive detention of suspects without trial for up to two years, arrest and search without a warrant, in camera, juryless trials with an unusually low burden of proof, and stricter control and censorship of the press. And black laws, from his viewpoint, "must be resisted to the utmost" (Khalil, 2016).

In essence, Law no. 6722 was also a black law that neither suspended fundamental rights nor granted extraordinary powers to the security forces. Instead, it retroactively created a "state of

---

28. Figures were mentioned by the Minister of Interior, S. Soylu, in a security meeting on 11 May 2018. See: https://www.icisleri.gov.tr/bakan-soylu-baskanliginda-istanbulda-secim-bolge-guvenlik-toplantisi-gerceklestirildi (Accessed: 16 8. 2018).

exception" through absolute legal immunity for security forces and a model for militarising law and order by deploying the Army "in aid of civil power".

Relying on the legal shield granted by Law no. 6722, special operation teams from the Army and Police, with the participation of the security guards (former provisional village guards), committed a semi-genocidal campaign and atrocities in the Southeast region of the country: some 2.000 people were reportedly killed in total between July 2015 and August 2016 while over 355.000 residents were displaced. Satellite image analysis, provided by UNITAR's Operational Satellite Applications Programme (UNOSAT), indicates that the damage caused by security operations in urban centres is commensurate with the use of heavy weapons and, possibly, air-dropped ammunition (OHCHR, 2017).

Since the abortive coup of 15 July 2016, Turkish security forces have been perpetrating horrific human rights abuses across the country: torture, extrajudicial execution, enforced disappearance, the use of lethal force against unarmed civilians and the forced displacement of residents. Such abuses mainly took place in Kurdish regions of the country under the 7/24 basis curfew conditions while thousands without any connection with the Gülen Movement, but targets of personal animosity or rumours were jailed or dismissed in the whole country.

Furthermore, hatred by the top guys of the regime through mass media also encouraged a process of civic degradation that left dissents vulnerable to aggression, mass killing, torture, disappearance and other forms of inhumane treatment. As NISA (2016) of Transparency International identified, such a regime relies on a "culture of impunity" where crimes committed by the army, the police and government officials are often left unpunished and are shown less reaction by the public.

All these campaigns led the Erdoğan regime to a new black law: right after the coup attempt, on 27 July 2016, Decree Law no. 668 was introduced. Article 37 of this decree grants absolute immunity in legal, administrative, financial, and criminal terms, for those who are taking decisions, performing duties, and involving actions in the scope of the decree laws issued under the SoE. This shall also be the norm retrospectively for officials already involved in repression of the coup attempt and subsequent terrorist activities. Public officials were thus provided *unaccountability* for their possible unlawful actions.

However, the story did not end there. So, one of the common features of the black laws is that they effectively place the security forces and vigilante groups, in their operations against civilians, beyond civilian oversight in legal sense. Erdoğan was ambitious to exempt his militant supporters in the streets from prosecution for their criminal behaviours including torture, kidnapping, and mass killings. The free movement of perpetrators in the public should be ensured while survivors are systematically kept at the stake.

To this end, on 24 December 2017, by article 121 of Decree Law no. 696, a sub-paragraph was inserted into article 37 of Decree Law no. 668. Within this paragraph, regardless of whether they have an official rank or they perform an official duty, as the norm for public officials, the government granted immunity to "civilians" who were deemed to have acted against the July 15 coup attempt and to those who acted to suppress subsequent terrorist activities. Immunity rule, leaving no room to bring perpetrators to court, has thus expanded to spontaneous vigilant acts of "patriotic" citizens (Table 7).

Table 7: Turkish Black Laws Enacted to Kill with Impunity

Laws/ D. Laws	Article	Scope	Rewards	Possible Result
6772	12	Army in aid of civil powers including security guards. Search without warrant. Usage heavy weapons	Judicial immunity for criminal acts performed by military personel. Prosecution is allowed by the superiors only.	Kill, injury, looting property, torture, inhumane tratement, disappearance in detention, solitary confinement. Wrongdoings and damages to people and property. Maladministration
668 (6755)	37	Enforcement of the decree laws by public officials and security forces.	Full judicial immunity. Prosecution disallowed.	
696 (7079)	121	Spontaneous vigilant actions of „patriotic" citizens.		
7145	26	Extentsion of the SoE conditions for a 3-year period. Extraordinary empowerment to governors	Limited prosecution for the crimes commited as related to the tasks, if the superiors allow.	Wrongdoings in dismissal, investigation, reinstates, snd other disenfranchisements.

Data Source: Turkish Official Gazette

Relying on this immunity package, as OHCHR (2018) found it, thousands of uncensored images of torture of alleged coup suspects in degrading circumstances were circulated widely in Turkish media and social networks after the coup, along with statements inciting violence against opponents of the regime. But artist and journalist Zehra Doğan was sentenced to two years and ten months in March 2017 on the basis of being part of an illegal "terrorist organisation" and "propaganda for the organisation" just because she depicted Nusaybin city as it was seen in an original photo *(See figure 12, page 225)*[29] while killers and torturers of 15 July have remained unpunished *(See figure 13, page 226).*

---

29. To be sure, for the referenced photo, see: https://www.dunyavegercekler.com/haber/38196-oz-yonetim-nusaybine-gomuldu.html (Accessed: 26 11. 2018).

Immunity rules within the black laws therefore make it – more or less – clear that the regime will not prosecute participation in the killing of "terrorists" or the plundering of their property, but rather encourage such vigilantes.

As a final point, all the black laws, when they enacted immunity for the criminals, create an **impunity effect** with which the state uses the criminal-justice system to absorb state-backed violence against dissents or minorities. M. Chatterjee (2017), with reference to judicial course of the anti-Muslim violence in Gujarat, India, in 2002, describes the impunity effect as a form of legality allowing the state "to inscribe, frame, and repackage violence to make it legally unaccountable" as well as reinforcing and deepening a form of state power based on the explicit subordination of minorities.

In that sense, the impunity effect is not the breakdown of the law, but is what the law itself imposed. Impunity effect makes you unable to overcome the perpetrators protected by the laws, to claim any financial redress for your damages, if you survived. Impunity, in other words, works "as a barrier to the recovery of survivors" (Rauchfuss and Schmolze, 2008).

Summing up, the crucial point concerning the proliferation of violence in any country is its impunity under the law. And Erdoğanist black laws best suit this logic of state terror in Turkey.

CONCLUSIONS

Central to this article is the conclusion that, through a trilogy comprising paramilitary death squads, SADAT-type service providers, and legal immunity for perpetrators, Erdoğan has developed his standards towards maintenance of the authoritarianism in Turkey. And now he seems to be prepared for the worst-case scenario: being overthrown, either by an election or coup. At least, we know he would respond to challenges to his tyranny with off-the-book operations.

Therefore, we think that the trilogy is tasked to defend the existing order against any worst-case scenario. Thus military attacks on the border regions of Syria are nothing more than an attempt to buy time for the Erdoğan regime to re-strategize his long-run political agenda. That is why Erdoğan has honoured certain common values like rule of law, democracy, freedoms, just in the breach.

Turning back to the *dispositifs* of M. Foucault in chapter 1, we can safely conclude that the regime, relying on the capacity of involving organised legislative operations, has distorted the juridico-legal system, disciplinary mechanisms and security apparatuses in the sense of responding to an emergency and organising relations of force (Dean, 2013), and thus lost its "economy of power." Removal of the norms does not lead to normality.

How the persecutions of the Erdoğan regime could evoke so little opposition, so much consent across the society and less sympathy for the victims, however, cannot be explained simply by a perplexity or fear of being punished by the regime. Such entails anthropological interrogations that could ultimately uncover the hatred and violence which became conflated with a decayed social order. As Rauchfuss and Schmolze (2008) put it clearly, a recovery of society under this culture of impunity is impossible.

The Erdoğan regime is in power today and seemingly immovable in the near future. Inside, its implicit source of support, rather than voters, comes from the political opposition remaining still in its comfort zone. Islamism and recently-engaged nationalism have also served as important sources of inspiration and intellectual support for his long-term agenda while the Turkish Left has offered very little in terms of a political vision of what that future might be like or how to get there.

Under these circumstances, what will happen remains to be seen in the course of the early election on **24 June**. But our expectation is that, rather than a non-competitive voting process, the Erdoğan era will expire when his foreign and domestic "enemies" combine their powers against him.

Until then, being aware that his crimes are not covered by the Presidential immunity, Erdoğan may officiate the exorcism séances at the Palace as well as playing the "shepherd-flock" game in the public sphere.

CHAPTER NINE

The end of constitutional government

*Things standing shall fall.
But the moving ever shall stay!*
Basavanna (1106 – 1167 AD)

LOSERS' CONSENT: "THE GUY HAS WON!"

IN THE EVENING OF 24 JUNE, THE DAY OF THE EARLY PRESidential and parliamentary elections, Turkish citizens heard the victory of Erdoğan from the mouth of his closest rival, Muharrem İnce of the CHP. He, left his supporters feeling betrayed by sharing his personal consent to the loss through *WhatsApp*, with a prominent journalist who was in a live performance at that time: "The guy [Erdoğan] has won" *(Adam [Erdoğan] kazandı!)*.[1] Many of us recall that, after İnce's message was broadcasted, the situation quickly turned in favour of Erdoğan.

Although he was able to capitalize on the almost apparent errors of Erdoğan and effectively mobilize supporters, İnce suddenly quit the scene with the reasons still unknown for public, sealing his rival's controversial victory. As an experienced figure of the Left wing, he showed very different consent to his loss.

---

1. See, for example: http://www.internethaber.com/muharrem-ince-adam-kazandi-video-galerisi-1 883 494.htm (Accessed: 26 June 2018). Readers may also recall that it was *Facetime* in the evening of the 15 July coup attempt as the communication app. marking the course of events.

Yet it was less clear whether we could credit his claim that the election was "not so much fraudulent."[2]

Thus, relying on the disappearance (!) of the suspicion regarding the fairness of the election, the Supreme Board of Election (YSK, a semi-judicial body in charge of management of electoral process in Turkey) could dare to announce electoral numbers. Figures and percentages were almost the same with those of the *Anadolu Agency* (AA), Turkey's state-owned news agency, as announced four days earlier than the election day in the form of "testing" accidentally appeared on some TV channels.

The YSK, on 4 July 2018, publicised the winner of the race with an 86.24 % voter turnout, Erdoğan taking 52.59 % of the vote against İnce's 30.64 %. The following day, the YSK, disregarding the previous presidents of the Republic of Turkey (12 in total including Erdoğan presided between 28 8. 2014 and 9 July 2018), declared Erdoğan, instead of "the 13th", as "the first" President of Turkey.[3] Erdoğan, ensuring immediate consent of the losers, as well as being in alliance with the Nationalist Action Party (MHP), won the election to succeed himself.

The other five candidates, however, somewhat remained silent, made no comment or posed no question on the results. They seemed to have accepted remaining in the playground as low profile figures, or they did not know how they must respond to their loss. Only one critic came from the free world: the OSCE (Organisation for Security and Cooperation in Europe), in its preliminary report (OSCE, 2018), found that the election

---

2. See, for example: https://www.amerikaninsesi.com/a/chp-secimlerde-hile-yok%CC%87/4 462 421.html (Accessed: 26 June 2018).
3. YSK Decision no. 2018/952 concerning the election results was published in the Official Gazette on 4 July 2018, with no. 30 468 (M). The following day, Decision no. 2018/954 sealing the Presidency of Erdoğan was also issued and published in the Official Gazette, with no. 30 469 (2ndM).

was held under the "restrictions on freedom of assembly, association and expression." To make it clearer, these restrictions were the normality of an ongoing SoE in the country. *(See figure 14, page 226)*

Furthermore, the OSCE (2018) identified the conditions lacking "equal basis" for contestants i. e. "restrictive legal framework and powers granted under the SoE limited fundamental freedoms of assembly and expression, including in the media [...] important legally prescribed steps were often omitted during counting and tabulation."

On the other hand, one of the presidential candidates, Selahattin Demirtaş of the pro-Kurdish HDP (People's Democratic Party) has been under arrest since November of 2016 on vague terrorism charges. He therefore had to campaign from a prison cell through Twitter messages shared by his advocates. Furthermore, the election campaign of HDP, particularly in western part of the country, took place in a climate of constant police and judicial intimidation.

As for Erdoğan, he was the most favoured candidate with excessive media coverage, misuse of state resources and usage of the SoE to restrict the freedoms of assembly and expression as identified by the OSCE (2018).

Recent elections in Turkey with the results well known in advance showed once again that, under the SoE or similar oppressive regimes, existence of multi-party elections is an illusion to a large extent and may not necessarily lead to multi-party democracy. Such kinds of elections rather serve to keep the façade of institutional democracy on behalf of the incumbent.

The guy won the last elections by passing from coercion to more subtle techniques of dominance rather than committing electoral frauds. The case of Muharrem İnce may give an insight into these "techniques" in the future. What distinguishes EAS from democracies is that electoral competition is rendered unfair or insufficiently free due to regime control and manipulation (Miller, 2017). As we learned from the OSCE report and from what İnce has not told us clearly, such was the case in the last elections of Turkey.

EXECUTIVE PRESIDENCY: "CHIEF EXECUTIVE PRESIDENT"

The Elections of 24 June produced a new type of "government" in July of 2018 that was literally seen to be embodied in the person of Erdoğan, sealing the transition from the parliamentary system to an "executive presidency" as supposed within the constitutional amendments that were narrowly adopted in the referendum of April 2017.

As such, 24 June represents a landmark in the history of modern Turkey, as it led to a country in turmoil: no checks, no balances, but discard of the bedrock constitutional principles by the "free" votes of the majority of citizens. So without seeing any problem to give up their will to the command of the one-person government, the majority of voters literally gave Erdoğan another five-year term as "executive" President, in addition to 15 years passed in his PM and the President of the Republic.

Thanks to the so-called executive presidential system that is highly customised to Turkey, Erdoğan is now answerable to no one since the system accommodates no constitutional machinery for controlling or balancing the executive powers. We then call the president of this system as "Chief Executive President" (CEP) which sounds a bit commercial. This also suits best with his following words in 2015: "The Republic of Turkey should be governed like a company!" (See chapter 7).

Of course, we are not yet in a position to fully grasp the new regime's *modus operandi* as it is likely destined to be a system-in-progress. What will happen remains to be seen, but what we witnessed here is the substitution of the government for the rule of Palace. And this book provided plenty of evidence showing that Erdoğan had already been captured by the tendency of governing the country as his "patrimonial property" i. e. like an estate inherited from his ancestors, rather than a company.

Furthermore, from the preliminary review of the new regime, we found significant evidences marking this tendency in the following areas: (1) normalisation of the SoE, (2) underestimation of the parliament, (3) concentration of the executive powers, (4) packing the judiciary with political appointees, and (5) subordination of the ruling party.

STATE OF EMERGENCY NORMALISED

In Turkey, the term "SoE" remained just a constitutional exception within the footnotes of textbooks and a less-applied regime for years. It has been taught in classes that the SoE was a regime in which the controls and guarantees of judicial order and certain fundamental rights can be suspended on the grounds that the country is in danger of falling into notable economic crisis, extensive natural or man-made disasters, anarchy, or dismantling.

The constitution, says that the SoE, is a provisional regime with a maximum duration of three-months, applied in an interval between two certain dates. However, the happenings since the coup attempt of 15 July have taught us that the SoE in which we lived was not the exception but a normalcy like the one established by Hitler right after the "Reichstag Fire".

The examples ranging from the brutality showed by the security forces for the sake of the "war on terror" to the Friday sermons *(Hutbe)* at mosques, round the clock curfews imposed even in small villages, forfeitures with no legal ground, arbitrary cancellation of passports, dismissals of civil servants without due process, shutting down of media outlets, mass arrests, unjust jailing, tortures, and solitary confinements during the SoE, also taught us how the state came to be present in the everyday life of people, how the state can penetrate into the ordinary life of its citizens and yet remain distant and elusive.

The SoE was declared on 21 July 2016, as a consequent reaction to the abortive coup of 15 July, and formally ended on 18 July 2018, so it was promised by Erdoğan in the last days of his campaign. Yet, as a just-in-case "measure" against any reversal, on 8 July 2018, just one day before the inauguration of the new government, 18.632 civil servants were dismissed by Decree Law no. 701. That was also the latest decree law issued under the SoE by the last cabinet of the parliamentary system.

However, reluctant removal of the SoE remained on the paper with two reasons: **First**, all decree laws in question were adopted by the TBMM (Table 8). Thus, they have gained some kind of "law" status and will continue to have effect even after the expiry of the SoE. This also implies that decrees involving disenfranchisements, some of which are listed in this book (chapter 4), remain forever unless legal amendments are made in the future. The AYM also cemented this continuity through decisions rejecting the suits filed by the main opposition party CHP, against the adopting laws.[4]

---

4. The AYM decisions were published in the Official Gazette of 30 June 2018, with no. 30 464 (1st and 2nd M).

Table 8: The Laws Adopting Decree Laws Issued under the SoE

#	No.	Decree Laws Publication Date	Publication No.	Law No.	Adopting Laws Publication Date	Publication No.
1	667	23 July 2016	29779	6749	29 Oct. 2016	29872
2	668	27 July 2016	29783 (2nd M)	6755	24 Nov. 2016	29898
3	669	31 July 2016	29787	6756	24 Nov. 2016	29898
4	670	17 Aug. 2016	29804	7091	8 Mar. 2018	30354 (M)
5	671	17 Aug. 2016	29804	6757	24 Nov. 016	29898
6	672	1 Sept. 2016	29818 (2nd M)	7080	8 Mar. 2018	30354 (M)
7	673	1 Sept. 2016	29818 (2nd M)	7081	8 Mar. 2018	30354 (M)
8	674	1 Sept. 2016	29818 (2nd M)	6758	24 Nov. 2016	29898
9	675	29 Oct. 2016	29872	7082	8 Mar. 2018	30354 (M)
10	676	29 Oct. 2016	29872	7070	8 Mar. 2018	30354 (M)
11	677	22 Nov. 2016	29896	7083	8 Mar. 2018	30354 (M)
12	678	22 Nov. 2016	29896	7071	8 Mar. 2018	30354 (M)
13	679	6 Jan. 2017	29940 (M)	7084	8 Mar. 2018	30354 (M)
14	680	6 Jan. 2017	29940 (M)	7072	8 Mar. 2018	30354 (M)
15	681	6 Jan. 2017	29940 (M)	7073	8 Mar. 2018	30354 (M)
16	682	23 Jan. 2017	29957	7068	8 Mar. 2018	30354 (M)
17	683	23 Jan. 2017	29957	7085	8 Mar. 2018	30354 (M)
18	684	23 Jan. 2017	29957	7074	8 Mar. 2018	30354 (M)
19	685	23 Jan. 2017	29957	7075	8 Mar. 2018	30354 (M)
20	686	7 Feb. 2017	29972 (M)	7086	8 Mar. 2018	30354 (M)
21	687	9 Feb. 2017	29974	7076	8 Mar. 2018	30354 (M)
22	688	29 Mar. 2017	30022 (M)	7087	8 Mar. 2018	30354 (M)
23	689	29 April. 2017	30052	7088	8 Mar. 2018	30354 (M)
24	690	29 April. 2017	30052	7077	8 Mar. 2018	30354 (M)
25	691	22 June 2017	30104 (2nd M)	7069	8 Mar. 2018	30354 (M)
26	692	14 July 2017	30124 (M)	7089	8 Mar. 2018	30354 (M)
27	693	25 Aug. 2017	30165	7090	8 Mar. 2018	30354 (M)
28	694	25 Aug 2017	30165	7078	8 Mar. 2018	30354 (M)
29	695	24 Dec. 2017	30280	7092	8 Mar. 2018	30354 (M)
30	696	24 Dec. 2017	30280	7079	8 Mar. 2018	30354 (M)
31	697	12 Jan 2018	30299	7098	8 Mar. 2018	30354 (M)
32	701	8 July 2018	30472	7150	3 Nov. 2018	30384 (M)

Data Source: Turkish Official Gazette (2016–2018)

Note: Decree Laws no. 698, 699, and 700 issued relying on Law no. 7142 are not present in the list as they fall out of the SoE regime.

Second, the TBMM adopted the Law no. 7145 aiming at broadening the influence of the SoE over the post-SoE as routine conditions of civic life "for a three-year period" as from the publication date of the law, 31 July 2018.[5] This means that the SoE will actually end on 31 July 2021 unless a new law is introduced to re-extend it.

Article 26 of Law no. 7145, keeping the standard provisions of the decree laws as they are, allows ministers and – at municipal level – governors to dismiss civil servants, workers, and military personnel arbitrarily, i. e. accusing them of being affiliated with the alleged terrorist organisations like the Gülen Movement without a judicial process as it was done by the decree laws during the SoE. For judges and prosecutors, however, it is the HSK and the relevant boards of the high courts who are authorised to do so. Academicians are decided to be dismissed by the Board of Higher Education (YÖK).

For the officials who dismissed or suspended (see chapter 2 for the term "suspension"), no deadline for the launch of investigation is applicable. They may then deem to be investigated or detained at any moment of this three-year pseudo-SoE period. In the investigation procedure, the minimum duration of suspension that is based on reasons other than alleged linkages with the Gülen Movement will apply for a one-year period while it is three months in usual suspensions.

All dismissals are followed by immediate cancellation of passports, annulation of ranks, vocational qualifications, and of gun licenses. As a practice of "guilt by association", passports belonging to spouses may also be cancelled by the Ministry of Interior if deemed risky for the general security.

As well as the overrule of the "individual criminal responsibility", Law no. 7145 ignores the principle of the "privacy" too when it comes to

> 1. *deposit accounts held by public officials, their spouses,*

---
5. Law no. 7145 was published in the Official Gazette of 31 July 2018, with no.30 495.

> *and their children at the Bank Asya (an interest-free bank shutdown for its alleged ties to the Gülen Movement): relevant authorities, i. e.* TMSF, *Banking Regulation and Supervision Agency (*BDDK*), and Financial Crimes Investigation Board (*MASAK*), are obliged to share all kinds of information and documents with the public institutions in which those officials are working. The restriction in article 73(1) of Law no. 5411 concerning "disclosure of the confidential information and commercial secrets" is not applicable in this respect.*
>
> 2. *All kinds of information and documents including communication through electronic devices i. e. cell phones, apps. downloaded etc. belonging to those who are being investigated because of "being affiliated with or connected to terrorist organisations or to organisations, entities or groups which the* MGK *had found to be engaged in activities harmful to the State" and their spouses, and their children: relevant authorities, i. e. Information and Communication Technologies Authority (*BTK*) and public/private entities are obliged to share the information and documents with the boards, commissions and other authorities in charge of investigation.*

On the other hand, TMSF, as the general trustee, continues to head the companies to which it was appointed during the SoE while legal provisions concerning the rights and responsibilities of TMSF representatives as individual trustees at these companies, and the affairs relating to asset values remain applicable until criminal investigation has been concluded or sales/liquidation process completed (see chapter 5).

Governors, for a maximum of a fortnight period, are authorised to ban the entry or exit of suspicious people into certain places in provinces in case of open danger concerning the public order and safety, and to ban meetings in certain streets and squares after the hours decided by the security services.

Prosecutors, having prior decision of the judgeship, are allowed to hold suspects in detention for up to twelve days (four days plus two extensions) for collectively committed crimes.

Looking at these samples of the restrictions, we can safely conclude that the issues and challenges have not changed substantially for "usual suspects" even in the post-SoE era of Erdoğan. Yet the constitutional framework that identifies the positions and powers of the core governance institutions, i. e. Legislature, Executive, and Judiciary, against each other has substantially altered.

LEGISLATURE UNDERESTIMATED

Thanks to the constitutional changes in the referendum of April 2017, Erdoğan also heads the ruling party, AKP, and sets the parliamentary agenda through decision-making processes working on the majority-voting basis. Therefore, the Grand National Assembly of Turkey (TBMM), although it was expanded to 600 MPs from 550, is not in a position to check the Palatial powers.

Actually, weaknesses in the checking mechanisms were not the matters that the country faced after the introduction of the constitutional changes. In 2016, a report by *Transparency International* evaluating the electiveness of Turkey's institutions in preventing and fighting corruption and in fostering transparency and integrity identified the key problem: "the failure to adequately separate powers and keep the executive in check.

[...] There is very limited constraint on the executive's power and official misconduct is rarely prosecuted and punished" (NISA, 2016). That is to say, the results of the referendum and the elections of 24 June both have baptised the authoritarian tendency that was already born.

Within the constitutional changes, all the executive powers that legislations had granted to the PM office and the Cabinet were replaced with the presidential authority. Such a replacement was also the case in the constitutional amendments with the following exception: provisions concerning the parliamentary supervision over the Cabinet and ministers, and approval of the laws on the budget and final account were removed from the article 87 of the Constitution.

These provisions were not translated into the parliamentary supervision over the presidential operations and corresponding expenditures. This obviously results in overrule of the "budget right" by the Palatial regime. As evidence, in lack of parliamentary approval for the budget proposal, the Constitution says the previous year's budget law will remain effective with the re-evaluated monetary figures (article 161). This, however, cannot be considered a "measure" balancing the Palatial power over the budgetary affairs but a kind of conferral giving way for the Palace to spend tax-payers' money in a discretionary manner.

As for the auditing mechanisms, the President cannot be asked any parliamentary question, whether oral or written. Just ministers and vice-presidents, namely secretarial figures of the Palace, are allowed to be inquired in a constitutional sense (article 98). The interpellation *(Gensoru)*, which may lead to an impeachment process, however, no longer exists as it was removed by the referendum of April 2017 (article 99).

Although they may seem a true combination of "checks and balances" at first glance, other nominal restrictions over the presidential authority should also be considered well-known Erdoğanist hoaxes. Let us review by some examples how such provisions work in practice:

The presidential authority Constitution disallows to issue decrees concerning human rights or overriding current laws (article 104): Courts, of course if any appeal occurs, will decide whether a decree overrules this restriction. Refer to the section below to see how the judiciary has been packed by the Palatial appointments.

Imagine that a presidential decree falling into dispute with the current laws or the TBMM adopts a counter-law on the same matter and this makes the former invalid according to the Constitution (article 104): Turkish administrative bodies are neither open to the notion of automatic invalidation nor authorised to settle conflicting provisions. They are used to work with the secondary/tertiary legislations like regulations, internal circulars, ministerial instructions, administrative orders etc. Then, who will decide that both are on the "same matter"? Courts again! Further, how could we imagine that the president will endorse the law beating his decree?

The presidential authority constitution prohibits submitting draft laws to the TBMM (article 88). At first glance, this seems to imply that the legislation process is driven by the MPs, not by the government as it was the case in the parliamentary system. Apart from the fact that political parties in Turkey often lack services to train MPs on their role in the legislature, this is just to create an illusion of separation between the legislative and executive branches because Erdoğan, as the leader of the parliamentary majority at the same time, is always able to translate the Palace-made drafts into laws while other bills get rejected regularly.

Think of an individual proposal passed "accidentally" without getting ex-ante consent of the majority leader: obviously, this will not be allowed to happen because Erdoğan likely sends this law back to the TBMM for reconsideration. In such a case, according to the constitutional change (article 89), the adoption of this proposal once again requires more than half of the absolute number of MPs, i.e. 301 out of 600, which possibly goes beyond the initial votes. For the MPs, to reach this *quorum* seems to be a low possibility.

Under the Turkish parliamentary democracy, the "presidential veto" was working just as a retardant factor against the will of the MPs' majority. But now, it makes the proposals very hard to be adopted once again and discourages coordinating efforts in this respect.

As these examples suggest, in the current distribution of the seats in the parliament a majority of which are being filled by the AKP and his nationalist ally MHP, those provisions just would serve to keep the façade of democratic institutions. In case of *co-habitation*,[6] however, such provisions may lead to a political crises that ultimately results in dissolving the TBMM together with early elections.

In conclusion, as a nominally democratic institution under the Palatial regime, the TBMM, lacking actual legislative power, is just there to pass Palace-made drafts to Erdoğan for endorsement. The TBMM may also serve as a controlled platform in which parties make their demands and negotiate with the Palatial regime over limited policy concessions.

---

6. In the literature, the term co-habitation refers to the governmental conditions of semi-presidential regimes under which the president and the prime minister are from different parties. I however use it here to describe the coexistence between a directly-elected president and a parliamentary majority holding political positions other than the president.

THE EXECUTIVE CONCENTRATED

Under the new regime, all the executive functions are to be led by the President from his Palace. The President appoints and dismisses his deputies (vice-presidents in undefined numbers, only one for the time being), ministers, governors, ambassadors, and high-level officials listed within the Presidential Decree no. 3 concerning the appointment procedures for the high-ranking officials.[7] The regime in which a PM and a "Council of Ministers" (the cabinet) no longer exist leaves no room to respective ministers to interfere in the appointment/dismissal process legally. The President does not take his decisions jointly, but on his own initiative.

Ministers in this system, individually or collectively, do not bear any political identity other than being the "Secretary of Palace." The Constitution (article 106) says both vice-presidents and ministers answer to the president, not to the parliament and just formally answer the oral and written questions directed by the MPs (article 98). The system transforms the ministries into fragile structures created by the presidential decrees and could therefore be removed suddenly by another decree. Such is not nominally, but substantially different from – for example – the "Secretary" of State, Defence, Treasury etc. in the presidential system of the United States.

Such loss of status is also the case for the "cabinet" or the council of ministers that is more than the sum of ministers: when Erdoğan gathers the ministers around a table this meeting no longer constitutes a "cabinet" in a governmental sense because the Constitutional articles 109 – 113 concerning the cabinet were removed by the referendum of April 2017. Widespread

---

7. Presidential Decree no. 3 was published in the Official Gazette of 10 July 2018, with no. 30 474.

usage of the term Cabinet *(Bakanlar Kurulu)* across Turkish mass media to describe such Palatial meetings is just a habitual usage, if not a distortion.

As for the governors, according to article 138 of Decree Law no. 703 amending article 9 of Law no. 5442 on the provincial governance, they are described as "the representative of the President and of his executive means in the province" (emphasis added). Governors, in the former article, had been designated as "the representative of the state and government and of each ministry."

The President, as the head of the Executive, has sole authority over the public institutions including the Army (i. e. appointment and promotion of the military staff and commanders) and Academia (i. e. appointment of the rectors including those of private universities) as well as having the power to dissolve the parliament, being able to declare a SoE for up to six months, and to appoint significant number of members to the high courts.

To this end, four substantial changes have been made in the parliamentary governance structure. **First**, relying on the empowerment granted by Law no. 7142, current legislations were adopted into the Palatial regime: within Decree Laws no. 698, 700, and 703, all the governmental sources of authorisation with reference to the terms "Prime Minister/Prime Ministry" or the "Cabinet (Council of Ministers)" within the current legislations were replaced with the term "President of the Republic."[8] Thus, these governmental structures coming from the Ottoman era lost their entities and were succeeded by the President while respective authorities were handed over to the Palace.

---

8. Law no. 7142 was published in the Official Gazette of 18 May 2018, with no. 30 425. Decree Law no. 698 was published in the Official Gazette of 4 July 2018, with no. 30 468 while Decree Laws no. 700 and 703 published on 2 July 2018 with no. 30 471 (2nd M) and no. 30 473 (3rd M), respectively. As these decrees were issued relying on the empowerment of Law no. 7142, they fall out of the SoE regime.

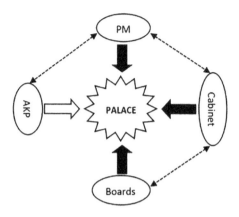

Figure 15: Transfer of Legal Authorities to the Palace (2018)
Note: Dotted lines represent the former governmental interactions in which (1) the PM was head of the Cabinet in the former system, (2) the General Chairman of the ruling party, and (3) Boards were advisory or complementary to the Cabinet in sectoral matters.

Second, all the current laws and decree laws founding the ministries were abolished by the Decree Law no. 703 or their titles referring to these ministries amended. For example, Law no. 6004 "Concerning the Establishment and Duties of the Ministry of Foreign Affairs" was named "the Law on Some Provisions Concerning the Staff at the Ministry of Foreign Affairs" (article 6) while Law no. 3154 "Concerning the Establishment and Duties of the Ministry of Energy and Natural Resources" was abolished (article 8).

And ultimately, by the Presidential Decree no. 1, consisting of 539 articles, new ministries – 16 in total – were re-established with slightly different names and duties than the previous ones[9] while the establishment of the affiliated institutions/agencies was put into force by the Presidential Decree no. 4.[10]

All the ministries were devised as the constituent parts of the "Presidential organisation." Over them, Decree no. 1

---

9. Presidential Decree no. 1 was published in the Official Gazette of 10 July 2018, with no. 30 474.
10. Presidential Decree no. 4 was published in the Official Gazette of 15 July 2018, with no. 30 479.

assigns nine "Palatial Boards" to certain sectoral areas: science, technology and innovation, education, economy, security and foreign policy, legal affairs, culture and art, health and food, social affairs, and local administrations (article 20). The boards with a minimum of three members to be directly assigned[11] by the President will be in charge of policy-making in these areas. Furthermore, the boards, each chaired by the President, are also vested with extensive power to oversee the ministries and relevant legal institutions in the context of the policies concluded.

Furthermore, granting each a "public legal entity" status with administrative and financial autonomy, article 525 of the Presidential Decree no. 1 establishes the four "Palatial Offices" to be working under the hierarchy of the President: (1) digital transformation, (2) finance, (3) human resources, and (4) investment (former Investment Support and Promotion Agency of Turkey). These offices are foreseen to work with a focus on long-term strategies and policy framework for key themes.

In practice, however, digital transformation refers to the coordinating efforts towards the transformation of the state into a *Panopticon*-like "digital state."[12] Human resource refers to the state-level coordination of the staffing and recruitment processes including selection exams in combination with the "intelligence services" provided by the MİT (see cataloguing of Chapter 4). Finance and investment offices, together or individually, signal the predatory operations over the markets and national resources to be led by the Palace.

Presidential Circulars no. 2018/7 disallowing the public

---

11. Presidential Decision no. 2018/196 concerning the appointment of 76 members to the Boards was published in the Official Gazette of 9 October 2018, with no. 30 560.
12. *Panopticon*: a type of institutional building and a system of control designed by the English philosopher and social theorist Jeremy Bentham in the late 18th century. The scheme of the design is to allow all (pan-) inmates of an institution to be observed (-opticon) by a single watchman without the inmates being able to tell whether or not they are being watched (Wikipedia, 2018).

institutions to employ any staff without getting ex-ante permission of the Palace, and no. 2018/8 putting the utilisation of the national real estates through sales, rent, allotment, transfer, truck etc. under the Palatial control, and no. 2018/10 designating the Ministry of Treasury and Finance, namely his son-in-law, as the coordinator in charge of decisions concerning the presidential "assignment" of the state-owned enterprises to certain operations – to be indemnified by the Treasury! – described in article 35 of the Decree Law no. 233, may give an insight to the readers.[13]

Third, the Presidential Circular no. 2018/3, as of 2 August 2018, transferred numerous duties and functions from the previous autonomous boards (19 in total) to the Presidential Palace, for example, macroeconomic planning, regional development, Money-Credit and Coordination, state aids, privatisation, cyber security, and so forth. Transfers are realised in two ways: direct reference to the person of the President or reference to relevant Presidential Offices.[14] Significant policy-making affairs concerning certain sectors have thus become involved with the Palace. Therefore, their existence cannot be traced directly within the semi-formal Palatial illustration, but from the Presidential decrees or decisions. *(See figure 16, page 227)*

Concisely, the governmental part of the Palatial regime appears to have become a system in which Boards and Offices determine the policy framework under the presidential leadership, while the ministerial structures are in charge of the implementation of these policies.

---

13. Presidential Circulars in question were published in the Official Gazette of 12 9. 2018, with no. 30 533, while the amendments in article 35 of Decree Law no. 233 were made within Decree Law no. 703 of 2 July 2018.
14. The Presidential Circular no. 2018/3 was published in the Official Gazette of 2 August 2018, with no. 30 497.

Table 9: Critical Institutions Affiliated / Linked to the Palatial Regime (2018)

Institutions	Affilation/ Linkage (Past)	Affilation/ Linkage (Today)	References
Radio & TV of Turkey (TRT)	Deputy PM in charge	Palatial Comm. Chairmanship	Presidential Circular no. 2018/2 (Linked)
National Intelligence (MIT)	Prime Ministry	President	Decree Law no. 694, Presidentia Decree no. 1
Saving Deposits Insurance Fund (TMSF)	Deputy PM in charge	President	Presidential Circular no. 2018/1 (Linked
Defence Industry (SSB)	Prime Ministry	President	Decree Law no. 696, Presidential Decree no 7
Turkey Wealth Fund (TWF)	Prime Ministry	President	Presidential Decree no. 1, Presidential Decisions no. 2018/162, 2018/163

Data Source: Turkish Official Gazette

Notes: (1) Other affiliated bodies in the Presidential Decree no. 1 are MGK, General Staff, Religious Affairs, State Archives, State Audit Board, National Palaces, Communication (former DG Press, Broadcasting and Information), and Strategy and Budgeting (some part of former Ministry of Development).
(2) Presidential Circular no. 2018/1 linking TMSF with the Palace was published in the Official Gazette of 15 July 2018, with no. 30 479.
(3) Presidential Circular no. 2018/2 linking TRT with the Chairmanship of the Palatial Communication was published in the Official Gazette of 24 July 2018, with no. 30 488.

Fourth, through various Palatial discretions, some critical institutions were affiliated or linked to the president himself or relevant presidential office. Presidential Decree no. 1, article 37, provides the list of "affiliated" institutions (11 in total) while Presidential Circulars make some legally autonomous institutions "linked" to the Palace (Table 9).

The MİT, when it was a semi-autonomous "undersecretariat" under the Prime Ministry, had already been brought under the control of Erdoğan by Decree Law no.694 of 25 8. 2017. As is known, according to the article 41 of this Decree, MİT was tasked with the "cataloguing" of military staff who may pose a threat to the regime (see chapter 4). Also, has MIT has been in the front and centre of the ongoing campaign to arm and resupply the *jihadist* terror groups. That was the case especially before and after the coup attempt of 15 July, and coordination of the Train-and-Equip Program against Assad of Syria (see chapter 8).

The TWF, as the "Sovereign Wealth Fund" of Turkey in its literature, was at the centre of wider discussions since its establishment in 2016. Presidential Decree no. 1, however, affiliating the TWF directly to the Palace, ended discussions while Presidential Decree no. 3 authorises the President to appoint its chairperson and members.

Erdoğan, relying on the presidential authority that is granted by himself, appointed himself (yes, himself!) to the post of the chairperson of the TWF executive board (Presidential Decision no. 2018/162), and his son-in-law, Berat Albayrak who is also the Minister of Treasury and Finance, as the deputy chairperson (Presidential Decision no. 2018/163). Namely, as from 12 9. 2018, Erdoğan will head the TWF and the national assets in its portfolio while the deputy is appointed by him (For further details, See chapter 6).

As for the SSB (Chairmanship of Defence Industry), Erdoğan's special interest in and prominent administrative design for this institution is also meaningful given that his other son-in-law, Selçuk Bayraktar of *Baykar Makine*, is among the leaders of the sector as the single source supplier of tactical UAVs and UCAVs (Unmanned Combat Aerial Vehicles) to the Army.

Erdoğan, as he promised in 2015 saying, "The Republic of Turkey should be governed like a company," has ultimately combined the governmental affairs with the "family business." The TWF and SSB are popular, but not the only evidence for this.

JUDICIARY PACKED

As is known, judiciary from high courts at the top to first instance courts at the bottom was targeted by the Erdoğanist government since the December 2013 corruption scandals. Since then, apart from the mass dismissal of 4.279 judges and prosecutors (see chapter 2), judicial organisations have gradually been put under the control of the Executive power through "legislative" operations and systematically left vulnerable to political intervention.

As a prominent example, just before the coup attempt of 15 July 2016, Law no. 6723 (articles 12, 22) was introduced in order to purge "blacklisted" members at the high courts.[15] Legally (!) ending the duration of the existing members in the chambers (a kind of dismissal indeed), HSK refilled the two high courts with new members who were considered to be pro-Erdoğan in critical files: 267 members to the Court of Cassation and 75 members to the Council of State, while Erdoğan appointed 24 members to the latter on ¼ basis.[16]

However, these changes appeared insufficient to serve the Palatial agenda concerning the judiciary and further changes became necessary in this vein: thanks to the constitutional amendments adopted by the referendum of April 2017, competitive elections for the membership of the HSK were replaced with the presidential and parliamentary appointments while the total number of the members dropped from 22 to 13.

Thus, the HSK, as a top judicial entity in charge of admission of the judges and prosecutors into the profession as well as

---
15. Law no. 6723 was published in the Official Gazette of 23 July 2016, with no. 29 779 (2nd M).
16. Appointment list for the Council of State was published in the Official Gazette of 29 July 2016, with no. 29 785; for the Court of Cassation: 30 July 2016, with no. 29 786; Presidential appointments to the Council of State: 27 July 2016, with no. 29 783.

their appointments, promotions, disciplinary proceedings, and dismissals, was put under the political power having serious potential to affect the decisions and choices made by the judicial order. That is the case particularly for penal courts purposely devised to intimidate dissents.

In the last days of 2017, however, within Decree Law no. 696,[17] total member seats in both civil and administrative high courts were increased: 100 new members to the Court of Cassation, 16 new members (of which four were appointed by Erdoğan) to the Council of State. Yet appointments came after the 24 June elections.[18]

Table 10: Changes in the Composition of the High Courts by Appointing Authorities

Judiciary	# of members		President		Parliament		HSK	
	Past	Today	Past	Today	Past	Today	Past	Today
AYM	17	**15**	14	**12**	3	**3**	0	**0**
Court of Cassation	310	**410**	0	**0**	0	**0**	310	**410**
Council of State	136	**152**	34	**38**	0	**0**	102	**114**
HSK	22	**13**	4+2	**4+2**	0	**7**	-	-

Data Source: Turkish Official Gazette, annual reports of the high courts

Notes: (1) The term "Past" principally refers to the numbers applicable before the adoption of the constitutional amendments by the referendum of 16 April 2017.
(2) The TBMM selects seven of the HSK members from among the members of the Court of Cassation (3), Council of State (1), and academicians in law and lawyers (3).
(3) In the past, 16 out of 22 HSK members were being selected by the general assemblies of the Court of Cassation (3), Council of State (2), Justice Academy (1), and the judges and prosecutors from among their eligible colleagues (10) while the President appoints four members.
(4) The Justice Academy of which the president is appointed by the cabinet decree

---

17. Decree Law no. 696 was published in the Official Gazette of 24 December 2017, with no. 30 280.
18. Appointments by Erdoğan and HSK were published in the Official Gazette of 17 July 2018, with no. 30 481.

was an institution subordinated to MoJ. The Justice Academy was shut down with the Decree Law no. 703 of 9 July 2018.
(5) The Constitution reckons the Minister of Justice and his undersecretary (vice-minister of today) as ex officio members of the HSK.
(6) President appoints the Council of State members on ¼ basis while HSK selects remaining the ¾ quota.
(7) Due to frequent fluctuations driven by the legislative operations, the numbers relating to the Court of Cassation and the Council of State still need to be confirmed.

Table 10 reveals the logic behind the appointment procedure surrendering the judiciary to the Palace. This logic runs like this: (1) Erdoğan, relying on both his own initiative and parliamentary majority led by himself, appoints all of thirteen HSK members. (2) Hence, the HSK members select the members of the two high courts. (3) High courts and YÖK – the members of which are also appointed by Erdoğan – nominate eight members to the Supreme Court, the AYM. (4) Erdoğan, in addition to his own four appointees, appoints these nominees while the parliamentary majority selects the remaining three from among the eligible candidates.

Needless to say, this closed circuit leaves almost no room for impartiality and a much lower degree of independence from the executive demands. And, without going into much more details, it can safely be concluded that the Turkish judicial system, from head to foot, has become highly politicized and reshaped through "legislative" operations in a way to better serve the Palatial agenda.

RULING PARTY SUBORDINATED

Changes in the Constitution (article 101) allow the president to be a party-member. Relying on this, the AKP congress of 21 May 2017 elected Erdoğan as the "General Chairman." As a "party-member president," he leads the AKP majority group in the TBMM and involves the daily party affairs ranging from chair of the boards to finalisation of the deputy/mayor candidate lists as well as appointment of the heads of local branches. He also attends events and meetings organised by the ruling party and its youth and women branches where he raises criticism against the leaders of the opposition before media and public.

Thus, the AKP of Erdoğan, enhancing its ability to invoke the values of patriotism, stability, faith, piety etc. , contributes to expand the Palatial hegemony beyond clientelist networks, while the majority group at the TBMM, acting as an arms-length machinery that is run to exclude the opposition from the law-making process, enables Erdoğan to influence the parliamentary agenda both in the general assembly and in the parliamentary committees where proposals are negotiated and finalised.

As such, the AKP appears not to be a "ruling party" but rather looks like the *cupbearer* of its ruler. Comparing to any opposing party, this makes the AKP vulnerable in the political realm. The AKP, in the future, may find itself ill-equipped to understand and adjust to the conditions when challenges to the *status quo* loom.

Whatsoever they wished to happen, a party-member president status has thus come to be replaced with a "partisan" president in a way to ensure Erdoğan's dominance over the legislative system. This replacement ultimately leads to an "electoral autocracy", a major trait of which is inability of the opposition to win elections due to structural disadvantages.

RULE OF LAW VS. RULE OF PALACE

In sum, the Erdoğanist system of government involving the complete placement of power – legislative, executive, and judicial – in one man to remake the political order, is one in which a Presidential top, which in fact corresponds to the Palace, is complemented by

1. a **parliament** *which of the main legislative agenda is dictated from the Palace through majority leadership represented by the president,*

2. **ministerial** *structures which are bound to the Palatial agenda through in-house Offices and Boards with no constitutional status,*

3. *a* **judiciary** *whose critical top organs are domesticated through Palatial and parliamentary appointments,*

4. *a ruling party, i.e.* **AKP**, *with many functions that are surrendered to the Palace through a "partisan" president, and*

5. **media** *outlets reflecting simply what the Palatial authorities have told them.*

As could be anticipated, the political organisation in this system depends highly upon the maintenance of personal relations between the president and household (Palace) members or "servants." The foundation of the constitutional order in Turkey is now the rule of the Palace and is incompatible with democratic governance.

Therefore, the organogram with a galactic appearance *(See figure 16, page 227)* does not display the actual work of the system and is to create an illusion of good governance. In essence, not referring to the level of hierarchical interactions between them from the vertical angle, it shows some formal players of the system from the top. Figure 17, however, is to disclose the inner view of the system from the eyes of a muckraker.

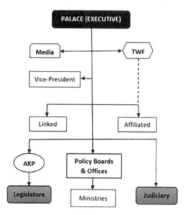

Figure 17: Overall Configuration of the Palatial Regime in Turkey
Note: Dotted lines illustrate not constitutional, but virtual controls.

This system illustrated above, disregarding the decentralising forces driven by the localities, tends to suppose the "concentration of the power in one hand" to be an effective decision-making capacity removing internal obstacles such as red-tapes and cumbersome, yet careful, bureaucratic working style frequently criticised by Erdoğan as a "bureaucratic oligarchy". Thus "quick responses to the challenges" e. g. economic reversals, foreign threats, and war on terror the country has faced in the last decades, would be given in that way.

Although it is doubtful that such an ambitious goal is sincerely adopted by Erdoğan, both in the referendum of April 2017 and snap elections on 24 June, the majority of citizens have endorsed his authoritarian instincts while the opposition, concerned scholars, and Turkey's Western allies argue that the system proposed would lead to a regime in which no checks and balances exist to keep the incumbent in line.

Erdoğan thus enjoyed absolute power over the state and took *responsibility* for "good governance" which includes the care and feeding (see chapter 4) of his – poor and elite – supporters, and maintenance of their cliental network with the Palace. What we really should concern, rather than disappearance of the PM office, issuance of decrees, and so forth, is that economy, institutions, authority, control, and surveillance apparatuses all moved to the Palace in an "irrecoverable" way.

I use the term irrecoverable – at least under the current political circumstances – to imply that counter-legislative initiatives that could be attempted in the future would not put the Erdoğanist authoritarianism in reverse, but an evolutionary process through which the Turkish society ascends to a contemporary state. I suggest that such a process associated with the following two contradictions can be observed through the prism of the *longue durée*.[19]

First, Erdoğan presented the changes leading to the so-called executive presidency as a "state-making" process whose midpoint is, in its turn, the Palace. He, moving the core governance structures from their historical/constitutional positions to the Palace, ultimately achieved to create his own "centre."

That is a state-making process with a particular refusal of the legacy of the previous parliamentary experiences and therefore the country backslides from modernity to *antiquity* where the first hierarchical and politically-centralised societies emerged (see below section).

Second, such a system in which the powers are concentrated

---

19. A concept developed by the prominent French historian F. Braudel (1902 – 1985) for social analysis in historical studies. *Longue durée* refers to the time of the long-term structures of social reality, the duration of one historical system. *In our cause, longue durée allows to interpret crisis as the possibility of fundamental structural change. For more information,* see Lee (2018).

within a Palatial complex – at least indirectly – degrades the legal entity of the state of which primary functions are gathered in the hands of one man as well as including the inability of public institutions to protect and secure the public interest, and their failure to struggle with the everyday problems to which they are assigned. Ultimately, these institutions will become less responsive to citizens' needs.

That is, at the same time, ironically a degradation process through which large institutions are divorced from the original functions that make them what they are and their aggregation would no longer be equal to a state. Thus, it translates the state-making process into a trend toward lower levels of citizen satisfaction with the performance of institutions because people ultimately discern that the "public" character of the institutions had already disappeared. However, this likely happens in the *longue durée* in which one needs a wider horizon to observe that the Palatial regime better extended to a contemporary government system.

One weak point from an organisational angle: although Erdoğan prefers hierarchy in power relations, the system includes no "hierarchy" in the sense of level of authorities combined with command and control mechanisms, but rather signals an "excessive concentration of power" at the Palatial level not in hierarchical but in arbitrary ways. That is like a physical *mass* that the collapse becomes inevitable when it reached the limits of its own capabilities. By the same token, the system, when overloaded, collapses under its own weight and becomes unsustainable but from a long-term perspective.

This also makes hierarchical relations "nominal" since the government, in a practical sense, exists by the Presidential decrees; the administrative system is therefore the sum of these decrees. In this type of systems, all critical decisions and actions, even some routine governmental activities will probably be postponed until the Palatial order has come into the picture.

For the foregoing reasons, I suggest that the Palatial regime would not have full control of the country through a power grasp. Therefore, when we infer meaning from the organograms above we must read the so-called presidential system as an attempt to exert authority, rather than as reflections of authority that were already a *fait accompli.*

If so, why are Erdoğan and his fellows in favour of this system? They favour it, because the concentration of power, creating an illusion of "comfort zone," serves to guarantee the viability and independence of the Palatial complex from the rest of society as well as financing the cliental relations through DUP activities. Being "independent from the rest" here refers to the inability of citizens to directly exert significant influence over government policy, as well as to receive protection from arbitrary action by governmental agents such as police, prosecutors, and so forth (Tilly & Tarrow, 2015). In a nutshell, that means moving the government away from the governed!

Therefore, we expect that the Palatial regime, as is shown within the previous chapters (see, for example, chapter 4 for the term "feeding"), would focus to collect significant national sources using a range of methods (i. e. forfeiture, predatory schemes, privatisations etc.) and subsequently mobilize those sources to specific political programmes. As is made explicit in chapter 7, this regime prefers predatory strategies of which payoffs are higher in a short-time perspective when it comes to making a choice between production and predation.

As for the matter of "quick response to the specific questions," it remains reduced to issuance of fresh decrees that can easily be replaced with the new ones in case of controversy or confusion that practitioners faced in the field. "Specific questions" in this respect, however, refer to the challenges imposing threat to the comfort zone in which Palatial elites feel safe.

On the other side, the regime, both at home and abroad, responds to socio-political challenges with a vulgar tone as if they were leading an archaic promiscuous human gathering evolving from stateless villages to complex polities. High appetite to regional conflicts that was significant for early state formations in an anthropological sense seems also relevant to this tendency. Furthermore, state-sponsored violence, both in urban and rural regions, still remains the hard kernel of modern Turkey. That is however almost the norm for many new-born states of the post-colonial era, not for relatively high-capacity states like Turkey.

RETURNING TO ANCIENT TIMES: GOVERNING WITHOUT GOVERNMENT

Findings of anthropologist Jason Ur (2014) concerning the cuneiforms from Ancient Mesopotamia where state formations first appeared showed that the most prominently missing word in the cuneiform documentation was a term for "the state" itself. Instead, a "palace" or specific rulers were mentioned by name or by title. Ancient Mesopotamian states are mainly represented by monumental buildings like palaces and temples, and this is compliant with their *archaic* form.

Furthermore, despite the existence of certain "official" duties, no general term for "office" or "officer" exists in Sumerian or Akkadian cuneiforms. This also seems to be reasonable for a body politic in which officials attained their positions by virtue of kinship proximity to king or ruling elites, and retained them through continual maintenance of those relationships (Ur, 2014). Findings imply that appointments were based on personal trust, not on technical qualification in the Weberian sense of the "patrimonial state" in which the most fundamental obligation of the subjects is the material maintenance of the ruler at the top.

These are strikingly identical with the major features of the Palatial regime of Erdoğan as we tried to demonstrate from the overall tone of the decrees as well as reflecting into the above-mentioned tables and figures. The regime in question refers neither to the State nor to the Public *per se*. Rather it refers to the President or to the Palace where he built the office as well as being resident therein. The concept of the state is not present in those decrees.

Such a regime embodied within the Palatial complex, rather than any contemporary presidential system like that of the United States, represents an archaic phase of state formation: maximum concentration of power at the centre of the structure that cannot be grounded on underdeveloped command and control apparatuses. From a historical perspective, body politics in which executive matters cannot be distinguished from daily "family business" of rulers are unique to Ancient states where "kinship" functions as a structuring principle to sustain strongly centralized political powers.

For all of these reasons above, we suggest calling this regime "Palatial" or Palace-state. As such, the Palatial complex in Turkey is an antithesis to the contemporary forms of the state and comparable only to its ancient samples in the Middle East. We also call this political system not a governmental, but an electoral "regime" with *autocratic* features in which the ruler governs without government. It is the "death of constitutional government" in a usual sense.

ELECTORAL AUTOCRACY: ONE THIRD OF DEMOCRACY!

Our analyses point to the conclusion that today's Turkey is clearly an undemocratic system of government and categorically falls into an "Electoral Autocracy" (EA) regime type like today's China, Russia, Azerbaijan, Kazakhstan, Egypt, Togo, Cameroon, etc. A regime is "undemocratic" to the extent that political rights are narrow and/or unequal, the consultation of citizens is minimal, and protections are fragile (Tilly, 2007).

As the term implies, EA regimes can be defined as "autocracies with legal multiparty competition for the legislature." What distinguishes them from democracies is that this electoral competition is rendered unfair or insufficiently free due to regime control and manipulation (Miller, 2017).

A. Schedler (2006), however, suggests a relatively exhaustive definition for EA regimes: "states under the control of a dictator who has successfully established the institutional facades of democracy, including regular multiparty elections for the chief executive, in order to conceal (and reproduce) harsh realities of authoritarian governance."

Miller (2017) developed a multinomial logit to predict transitions to EA and democracy from a sample of closed (non-electoral) autocracies from 1946 – 2010. However, the transition from an electoral democracy to an EA as the case in today's Turkey remained less examined and a bit theoretical. Many still prefer to study well-known historical examples such as Germany of Hitler, Italy of Mussolini etc. This chapter therefore suggests that Erdoğan's Turkey could also be taken as a case study to illustrate how an electoral democracy was transformed into an EA regime within a decade.

As Erdoğan took over an electoral democracy with some flaws in the last days of 2002, it was not easy to turn Turkey into a perfect autocracy. For him, EA was a reluctant but strategic choice driven by the fact that economic-financial ties to the EU countries and the United States make the country vulnerable to the influences of the Western democracies as well as the norms and standards promoted by the international organisations like IMF, World Bank, OECD, WTO etc. As such, the Palatial regime in Turkey seems destined to be an unfinished project until conditions of perfect autocracy have prevailed.

Yet, through frequent referenda, elections, displays of piety, and even an abortive coup, Erdoğan has ultimately turned the state into a one-person government. As detailed above, the government was removed and all the executive powers gathered at the Palace while the judiciary was packed by political appointments. However, one remaining part of the Turkish democracy i. e. Legislature involving parties competing in elections, still plays a role in the rite of governance, despite some significant injuries. Then, we can assume that the Palatial regime provides citizens with one third of a democracy, "one third – democracy" in sum!

At that point, readers may ask the following: Erdoğan as an authoritarian ruler, while he systematically attempts to degrade the governmental structures – if not entirely, distorting their public characters – in one side, why does he still continue to govern with nominally democratic institutions, i. e. parliament and political parties including his so-called ruling party, the AKP? Because, as Gandhi (2008) correctly observed, legislative and partisan institutions remain important components in the operation and survival of authoritarian regimes. In other words, it is a delusion to think that dictators or autocrats do rule alone. They govern with institutions that are particular to their type. They may even have "nominally democratic institutions" such as a parliament and political parties.

Nominally democratic institutions provide autocrats with a democratic façade because of their "electoral nature" and function as instruments of co-optation that can be used by the rulers to address some basic governance problems. In general, scholars have analysed these problems from the angle of the three interrelated factors: (1) legitimacy, (2) risk management, and (3) economic survival.

Legitimacy: autocrats across the globe hold elections as a means of legitimizing the *status quo* in the eyes of both domestic and international actors (Magaloni, 2010). However, this particularly is the case when conditions dictate that authoritarian rulers must do so. For example, when motivated by international pressure and/or domestic legitimacy, elections may satisfy a normative or prescriptive demand by observers (Schedler, 2006).

Most importantly, autocrats strategically need a screen of fair-play with a variety of losers' consent enabling him to argue that no flaw exists within the electoral system. To this, they should be kept alive in the political realm. As William H. Riker rightly observes, without the losers we do not get to play the game (Anderson *et al.*, 2005). Such also functions to create an appearance that autocrats can point to as evidence of their democratic credentials. Of course, in today's Turkey, it is Erdoğan who knows this best.

Risk management: regular elections under tightly controlled party competition allows rulers of authoritarian regimes to effectively monitor their country's elites, the state apparatus, and the citizenry, thus averting risks of the regime's sudden collapse due to domestic political conflicts (Geddes, 2005). Since even heavily manipulated elections present a genuine threat, autocrats are more likely to adopt contested elections if they anticipate that they can reliably win them. In the latter scenario, elections may promote a regime survival through domestic political advantages, either by co-opting elites into the party hierarchy or extending control over citizens (Miller, 2017). Parliaments and parties may also serve to neutralize threats to his rule. He may offer a mix of carrots and sticks like repressing some and co-opting others (Gandhi, 2008).

Economic survival: autocrats recognize that a range of international benefits financial assistance, trade, and military alliances that are nominally targeted at "democracy" promotion can be secured with merely contested elections. As a result, they strategically adopt flawed elections and reap the rewards. M. K. Miller (2017), in his multinomial logit model, demonstrates that "economic engagement with democracies" strongly encourages the authoritarian rulers toward EA, but the effect on democratization is slightly negative.

Miller also argues that the socio-economic factors are generally unrelated to democratization, but strongly predict EA transition. However, the effects go in the opposite direction of what one would expect from the democracy literature: autocracies are more likely to adopt multiparty elections at *low* economic development and *high* inequality (Miller, 2017). That is highly explanatory for the major outcomes of the macroeconomic policies that have been adopted by the AKP governments within the last decade of Turkey (see chapter 7).

OPPOSITION: LOSING GROUND OR LEADING CHANGE?

When it comes to the opposition parties, they likely failed to assess correctly why they were losing in every election, or they gave consent to be governed by the Palace in advance. Some signals that we touched upon at the beginning of this chapter acknowledge this tendency.

The two-round electoral system opens some possibilities for presidential candidates to use the first-round results to gauge their level of support and cut deals. However, the opposition parties, despite some attempts to ensure cohesiveness, failed to evaluate the chance for a run-off to be held between the two best-performing candidates.

While EA regimes use elections to legitimate their rule, identify opponents, and reward allies with political patronage, opposition can also evaluate these elections as a legitimate institutional umbrella for activism, often around the theme of electoral fraud (Anderson et al. , 2005). However, amidst intensive electoral frauds some of which were even identified by the OSCE (2018), what played the role in mediating Turkish opposition leaders' sense of loss still remains secret. They neither challenged the results in unison nor contested them through legal processes or massive mobilizations.

As such, Turkish opposition leaders, rather than being losers of the recent elections, seem to be losers of motivation for change, as well as setting an *antithesis* which is essential in the political realm. Nevertheless, from an optimistic point of view Anderson *et al.* (2005) quoted from Riker, "the dynamics of politics is in the hands of the losers. It is they who decide when and how and whether to keep on fighting. Winners have won and do not immediately need to change things. But losers have nothing and gain nothing unless they continue to try to bring about new political situations. This provides the motivation for change." A lack of such a motivation therefore sustains losing and does not attract new voters.

In a wider sense, the Turkish opposition's future seems to depend largely on its ability to mobilise the masses towards repressive policies of the Palace. In this vein, what the opposition needs, however, is less theory but more practice, zero consent to the will of incumbent.

Lastly, when saying "Opposition," I do mean the Turkish Left that has offered very little in terms of a political vision of what that future might be like or how to get there, not the parties of the right-wing having no ethics of opposition. *(See figure 18, page 227)*

As far as the dissents are concerned, they all must have come to realise that neither incumbent nor opposition parties will ever genuinely defend their interests. That was why, despite the expiry of the SoE, further crackdowns have been introduced within Law no. 7145 (see above) against the growing confidence that street protests would influence politics and make their demands heard.

CONCLUDING REMARKS

Analysing the constitutional changes and combining them with the authoritarian tendency that has reached its top during the two-year SoE period, we can safely identify today's Turkey as a country where legislature was gutted, the judiciary was put under the Palatial tutelage, and executive power is gathered at the Palace. The relevant literature across the political science partly referred to within this book considers such a regime "Electoral Autocracy." Taking the physical – and popular – centre of the power into consideration, we call it Palatial Regime.

The main advantage of this regime is that, thanks to the large mass of poor people who can be co-opted through clientelism and state assistances, "the Guy" of Muharrem İnce, Erdoğan, is vulnerable to a minimal risk of being the loser. Furthermore, "the bureaucratic rationality of the state can always evoke the very facts of its illegibility to the poor as the major form of its defence" (Das, 2004). Many bureaucratic failures or illegitimate uses of force can thus be explained with reference to the conditions under which the poor are systematically kept: they are illiterate, uneducated, tend to panic, and so on. Wealthier citizens, however, are more difficult to treat as such.

The second advantage is the fact that the divides in society are characterised by ideologically-driven conflicts to a large extent. As Blanton and Fargher (2008) simply put it, under these circumstances, individuals feel no social impetus to develop a sense of *self* that could be the basis for heterodox social action such as opposition to the State and its policies enforced by the governmental agents. This kind of social environment favours the growth of authoritarian regimes able to assert total power over passive subalterns.

Briefly, both advantages are the ones leaving less need to further ones. That is to say, an autocrat in Turkey will only need to (1) keep poor citizens as they are through gastro-political tactics and religious narratives, and (2) to provoke the ideological conflicts and divides across society.

However, this regime dialectically accommodates its inner weaknesses that can be interpreted as the strongest predictor of democratization over the long-term: First, the regime is weak *per se* as it places the Palace at the top. But his top rises above a deserted bottom i. e. the institutions that have haemorrhaged significant human resource to the recent occurrence of an abortive coup and been degraded through a novel organogram putting some virtual boards and offices over them. The organogram implies that a "quick response to specific questions" will be formulated by the Palatial bureaucracy, instead of good governance with some participatory mechanism.

Secondly, the recent presidential election dramatically increased the cost for Erdoğan to lose since the political survival of him and his entourage was at stake. Therefore, he has become highly dependent on the Palatial regime to create additional incentives to hold power at any cost. If not, no second best is there for Erdoğan, no excuse particularly in case of failure to run the economy in a proper way.

As the state and government both became literally embodied in the person of Erdoğan, avoiding prophetic statements, we can assume that an electoral loss may give way to a re-democratisation of the country. That is why he tries to domesticate and intimidate the opposition on the one hand, systematically widens the scope of the regime's political edge to various parts of society on the other.

The third weakness, however, ironically stems from the "high capacity" of the country in governmental sense. Regardless of being governed by a democratic or undemocratic regime, Tilly and Tarrow (2015) consider Turkey among relatively high-capacity regimes. In this regime type, when a high-capacity government intervenes in population, activity, and resources, it makes a big difference; it raises taxes, distributes benefits, regulates traffic flows, controls the use of natural resources, and much more. Low-capacity governments may try to do the same things, but they have little effect. The Erdoğan-led Palatial regime may not easily waste this capacity because such needs "capacity" too.

Thanks to the case of Turkey, we have also experienced what Tilly and Tarrow (2015) suggest in the context of the political processes in which relatively extensive democratic institutions were overturned by the fascist and state socialist regimes to high-capacity undemocratic rule: "nothing guarantees that democratic institutions will stay in place forever." On the contrary, they need to be defended by not only the opposition parties but also "civil society" as a whole. States become vulnerable to de-democratization when they have lost their capacity through widespread violence driven by wars, terror, coups, and deepening social fragmentation.

Finally, instead of blaming the poor, we should develop a new understanding of the nature of poorness while studying the struggle with poverty. I suggest here that it is society rather than governments that ought to concern itself with poverty. As a global trend, the increasing need for institutionalised forms of organisation and related growth of governmental interventions reinforced the sense of vulnerability for many poor and, to some extent, middle-income households. This could be inverted through a widening "safety net" to be underwritten by the whole of society.

As for religions and ideologies which cannot comprise the ethical domain *per se*, especially when honoured by the incumbent, they do nothing other than serving to veil the unequal distribution of the benefits and the costs among citizens. Promoting ethics and humanitarian values against their outcries, the civil society in general, social movements in part, can sustain democratic institutions.

The point is clear: The Turkish society cannot construct a civilization characterised with a prominent palace. Palatial civilisations already remained in ancient times, and today the mottos like "Palace of Nation", "Garden of Nation" etc. merely reflect hegemonic ambitions of greedy rulers.

***

REFERENCES

Agamben, G. (1998). *Homo Sacer: Sovereign Power and Bare Life.* D. Heller-Roazen (Trans.). Stanford, CA: Stanford University Press.

Amnesty International (2018). *Purged Beyond Return: No Remedy for Turkey's Dismissed Public Sector Workers.* London, UK: Amnesty International Ltd.

Anderson, C. J. , Blais, A. , Bowler, S. , Donovan, T. & Listhaug, O. (2005). *Losers' Consent: Elections and Democratic Legitimacy.* New York: Oxford University Press.

Angeletopoulos, G. A. (2008). *The Turkish Capital Tax (Varlık Vergisi): An Evaluation.* Retrieved from: https: //ejournals. epublishing. ekt. gr/index. php/deltiokms/article/viewFile/2648/2413. pdf (Accession: 20 8. 2017).

Appadurai, A. (1981). Gastro-politics in Hindu South Asia. *American Ethnologist, 8*(3), 494 – 511.

Backer, L. C. (2015). International Financial Institutions (IFIs) and Sovereign Wealth Funds (SWFs) as instruments to combat corruption and enhance fiscal discipline in Developing States. *International Review of Law,* 2015: swf.5

Beety, V. E. , Aloi, M. & Johns, E. (2015). Emergence from Civil Death: The Evolution of Expungement in West Virginia. *West Virginia Law Review, 117*: Online 63.

Bhagwati, J. N. , Brecher, R. A. & Srinivasan, T. N. (1984). DUP Activities and Economic Theory. *European Economic Review, 24,* 291 – 307.

Blanton, R. & Fargher, L. (2008). *Collective Action in the Formation of Pre-Modern States.* New York, NY: Springer.

Boix, C. (2003). *Democracy and Redistribution.* New York, NY: Cambridge University Press.

Bortolotti, B. , Fotak, V. & Megginson, W. L. (2014). *The Rise of Sovereign Wealth Funds: Definition, Organization, and Governance.* Baffi Center Research Paper No. 2014 – 163.

Bratton, M. & Masunungure, E. (2011). The Anatomy of Political Predation: Leaders, Elites and Coalitions in Zimbabwe, 1980 – 2010. *The Developmental Leadership Program,* Research Paper 09.

Burkart, J. M., Brügger, R. K. & van Schaik, C. P. (2018). Evolutionary Origins of Morality: Insights from Non-human Primates. *Frontiers in Sociology*, 3, 17.

Campbell, B. B. (2002). Death Squads: Definition, Problems, and Historical Context. In B. B. Campbell & A. D. Brenner (Eds.), *Death Squads in Global Perspective: Murder with Deniability* (pp.1 – 19). New York, NY: Palgrave Macmillan.

Chatterjee, M. (2017). The Impunity Effect: Majoritarian Rule, Everyday Legality, and State Formation in India. *American Ethnologist*, 44(1), 1 – 13.

Chin, G. J. (2012). The New Civil Death: Rethinking Punishment in the Era of Mass Conviction. *University of Pennsylvania Law Review*, 160, 1789 – 1833.

Cornelius, D. (2008). Are Sovereign Wealth Funds State-Owned Enterprises? Retrieved from: http://www.compliancebuilding.com/2008/11/04/are-sovereign-wealth-funds-state-owned-enterprises/ (Accession: 28 9. 2017).

Couto, R. A. (2010). The Politics of Terrorism: Power, Legitimacy, and Violence. *Integral Review*, 6(1), 63 – 81.

Çubukçu, S. (2018). *The Rise of Paramilitary Groups in Turkey*. Retrieved from: http://smallwarsjournal.com/index.php/jrnl/art/rise-paramilitary (Accession: 23 May 2018).

Das, V. (2004). The Signature of the State: The Paradox of Illegibility. In V. Das & D. Poole (Eds.), *Anthropology in the Margins of the State* (pp.225 – 252). New Delhi: Oxford University Press.

Das, V., Poole, D. (2004). State and its Margins: Comparative Ethnographies. In V. Das & D. Poole (Eds.), *Anthropology in the Margins of the State* (pp. 3 – 33). New Delhi: Oxford University Press.

DAV (2018). *Turkey and the ECtHR: (In)effective Remedies from Strasbourg*. A Conference Report by the German Bar Association (Deutscher Anwaltverein, DAV). Retrieved from: http://www.eldh.eu/fileadmin/user_upload/ejdm/publications/2018/DAV_Conference_Report_-_Turkey_and_the_ECtHR (Accession: 5 August 2018).

Dean, M. (2013). *The Signature of Power: Sovereignty, Governmentality and Biopolitics*. Thousand Oaks, CA: SAGE.

Dedeoğlu, E. (2017). *What Can Turkey's Sovereign Wealth Fund do with this Portfolio?* Ankara, TR: The Economic Policy Research Foundation of Turkey (TEPAV).

Dery, A. W. (2012). *Overview of Asset Forfeiture*. Retrieved from: https://www.americanbar.org/publications/blt/2012/06/02_dery.html (Accession: 20 8. 2017).

Dzehtsiarou, K. , Greene, A. (2011). Legitimacy and the Future of the European Court of Human Rights: Critical Perspectives from Academia and Practitioners. *German Law Journal*, *12*(10), 1707–1715.

Eissenstat, H. (2017). *Uneasy Rests the Crown: Erdoğan and 'Revolutionary Security' in Turkey*. Washington, DC: POMED (Project on Middle East Democracy).

European Commission (2018). *Commission Staff Working Document: Turkey 2018 Report*. Brussels: European Commission. Retrieved from: https://ec.europa.eu/neighbourhood-enlargement/sites/near/files/20 180 417-turkey-report.pdf (Accession: 12 October 2018).

European Commission (2009). *Assessing the Effectiveness of EU Member States' Practices in the Identification, Tracing, Freezing and Confiscation of Criminal Assets (Final Report)*. Brussels: Matrix Insight.

Evans, P. B. (1989). Predatory, Developmental, and Other Apparatuses: A Comparative Political Economy Perspective on the Third World State. *Sociological Forum*, *4*(4), Special Issue: Comparative National Development: Theory and Facts for the 1990 s, 561–587.

FAC (2017). *The UK's Relations with Turkey (Tenth Report of Session 2016–17)*. London: Foreign Affairs Committee (FAC) of the House of Commons. Retrieved from: https://publications.parliament.uk/pa/cm201 617/cmselect/cmfaff/615/615.pdf (Accession: 7 August 2018).

Ferguson, N. & Burgess, M. (2009). From Naivety to Insurgency: Becoming a Paramilitary in Northern Ireland. In D. Canter (Ed.), *The Faces of Terrorism: Multidisciplinary Perspectives* (pp.19–33). West Sussex, UK: Wiley-Blackwell.

Frayne, D. (1999). *Sargonic and Gutian Periods (2334–2113 BC)*. Toronto: University of Toronto Press.

Freedom House (2018). *Democracy in Crisis: Freedom in the World 2018*. Retrieved from: https://freedomhouse.org/sites/default/files/FH_FITW_Report_2018_Final_SinglePage.pdf (Accession: 11 11. 2018).

Gandhi, J. (2008). *Political Institutions under Dictatorship*. Cambridge, UK: Cambridge University Press.

Geddes, B. (2005). *The Role of Elections in Authoritarian Regimes*. Washington, DC: Paper presented at the annual meeting of the American Political Science Association (APSA).

Holtgen, D. [@COEspokesperson]. (2018, May 24). Criticism of the European Court of Human Rights' handling of #Turkish post-coup cases is ill-informed and counterproductive. The #ECHR will not be pressurised by anyone [Tweet]. Retrieved from: https://twitter.com/COEspokesperson/status/999652901822877696

IMF (2013). *Sovereign Wealth Funds: Aspects of Governance Structures and Investment Management.* IMF Working Paper No.13/231 prepared by A. Al-Hassan, M. Papaioannou, M. Skancke, and C. Chih Sung.

İnce, B. (2012). *Citizenship and Identity in Turkey: from Atatürk's Republic to the Present Day.* London: I. B. Tauris.

Inda, J. X. (2005). Analytics of the Modern: An Introduction. In J. X. Inda (Ed.), *Anthropologies of Modernity: Foucault, Governmentality, and Life Politics* (pp.1–20). Malden, MA: Blackwell.

Khalil, T. (2016). *Jallad: Death Squads and State Terror in South Asia.* London: Pluto Press.

Kramer, M. (2015). *Understanding Predatory Leadership: The First Step toward a World Free of War, Corruption and Poverty.* Retrieved from: http://impada.org (Accession: 5 February 2018).

van der Kroef, J. M. (1987). Terrorism by Public Authority: The Case of the Death Squads of Indonesia and the Philippines. *Current Research on Peace and Violence, 10*(4), 143–158.

Kurer, O. (2002). Why do Voters Support Corrupt Politicians? In A. K. Jain (Ed.), *The Political Economy of Corruption* (pp.63–86). London: Routledge.

Lee, R. E. (2018). Lessons of the Longue Durée: The Legacy of Fernand Braudel. *Historia Crítica, 69*(2018), 69–77. doi: https://doi.org/10.7440/histcrit69.2018.04

Lever, M. D. (2015). A Person of Interest: Gordon Childe and MI5. *Buried History, 51,* 19–30.

Levi, M. (1988). *Of Rule and Revenue.* Berkeley, Los Angeles, CA: University of California Press.

Lundahl, M. (1997). Inside the Predatory State: The Rationale, Methods, and Economic Consequences of Kleptocratic Regimes. *Nordic Journal of Political Economy, 24,* 31–50.

Magaloni, B. (2010). The Game of Electoral Fraud and the Ousting of Authoritarian Rule. *American Journal of Political Science, 54*(3), 751–65.

Martín-Baró, I. (1989). Political Violence and War as Causes of Psychosocial Trauma in El Salvador. *International Journal of Mental Health, 18*(1), 3–20.

Mason, T. D. & Krane, D. A. (1989). The Political Economy of Death Squads: Toward a Theory of the Impact of State-Sanctioned Terror. *International Studies Quarterly, 33*(2), 175–198.

Mazzei, J. (2009). *Death Squads or Self-defense Forces? : How Paramilitary Groups Emerge and Threaten Democracy in Latin America*. Chapel Hill: The University of North Carolina Press.

McGregor, E. K. (2009). Confronting the Past in Contemporary Indonesia. *Critical Asian Studies, 41*(2), 195–224. doi: 10.1080/14672710 902 809 351

Meyer, K. , Tope, D. , & Price, A. M. (2008). Religion and Support for Democracy: A Cross-National Examination. *Sociological Spectrum, 26*(5), 625–653.

Milhench, C. (2017). *A new breed of sovereign wealth fund – without the wealth*. Retrieved from: http: //www. reuters. com/article/us-emerging-swf-investment/a-new-breed-of-sovereign-wealth-fund-without-the-wealth-idUSKBN16R0QY (Accession: 28 9. 2017).

Miller, B. L. & Spillane, J. F. (2012). Civil death: An Examination of Ex-Felon Disenfranchisement and Reintegration. *Punishment & Society, 14*(4), 402–428.

Miller, M. (2017). Strategic Origins of Electoral Authoritarianism. *British Journal of Political Science*, 1–28. doi: 10.1017/S0007123 417 000 394

Montesquieu (2008)[1721]. *Persian Letters* (Trans. M. Mauldon). New York: Oxford University Press.

Morack, E. (2018). Turkifying Poverty, or: the Phantom Pain of İzmir's Lost Christian Working Class, 1924–26. *Middle Eastern Studies (AOM, to be published in 2019)*.

NISA (2016). *National Integrity System Assessment (NISA) – Turkey (April 2018)*. Transparency International-Turkey. Retrieved from: https: //www.transparency. org/whatwedo/publication/national_integrity_system_assessment_turkey_2016 (Accession: 19 October 2018).

OHCHR (2017). *Report on the human rights situation in South-East Turkey (July 2015 to December 2016)*. Geneva: Office of the United Nations High Commissioner for Human Rights (OHCHR).

OHCHR (2018). *Report on the impact of the state of emergency on human rights in Turkey, including an update on the South-East*. Office of the United Nations High Commissioner for Human Rights (OHCHR).

OSCE (2018). *International Election Observation Mission: Republic of Turkey, Early Presidential and Parliamentary Elections, 24 June 2018*. Statement of

Preliminary Findings and Conclusions by the Organisation for Security and Cooperation in Europe (OSCE). Retrieved from: https://www.osce.org/odihr/elections/turkey/385 671? download=true (Accession: 26 June 2018).

Rauchfuss, K. & Schmolze, B. (2008). Justice Heals: The Impact of Impunity and the Fight against It on the Recovery of Severe Human Rights Violations' Survivors. TORTURE, *18*(1), 38–50.

Robinson, J. A. (1999). *When is a State Predatory?* CEsifo Working Paper No.178, Center for Economic Studies and Ifo Institute (CEsifo), Munich.

Russell, S. A. (2005). *Hunger: An Unnatural History*. New York, NY: Basic Books.

Saunders, H. D. (1970). Civil Death – A New Look at an Ancient Doctrine. *William & Mary Law Review*, *1*(4), 988–1003.

Schedler, A. (Ed.) (2006). The Logic of Electoral Authoritarianism. *Electoral Authoritarianism: The Dynamics of Unfree Competition* (pp.1–23). Boulder, CO: Lynne Rienner Publishers.

Schwarcz, S. L. & Rothman, A. E. (1993). Civil Forfeiture: A Higher Form of Commercial Law? *Fordham Law Review*, *62*, 287–320.

Semelin, J. (2007). *Purify and Destroy: The Political Uses of Massacre and Genocide (Trans. by C. Schoch)*. New York, NY: Columbia University Press.

Shumba, J. M. (2016). *Zimbabwe's Predatory State: Party, Military and Business Complex* (Doctoral dissertation). Johannesburg, SA: University of Witwatersrand.

Silva, S. (2013). Reification and Fetishism: Processes of Transformation. *Theory, Culture & Society 30*(1), 79–98. doi: 10.1177/0263276 412 452 892

Sluka, J. A. (2000 a). Introduction: State Terror and Anthropology. In J. A. Sluka (Ed.), *Death Squad: The Anthropology of State Terror* (pp.1–45). Philadelphia, PA: University of Pennsylvania Press.

Sluka, J. A. (2000b). "For God and Ulster": The Culture of Terror and Loyalist Death Squads in Northern Ireland. In J. A. Sluka (Ed.), *Death Squad: The Anthropology of State Terror* (pp.127–157). Philadelphia, PA: University of Pennsylvania Press.

Smith, G. S. (2015). *Guilt by Association: Heresy Catalogues in Early Christianity*. New York, NY: Oxford University Press.

SoS (2017). SADAT: *Erdoğan's Private Army*. A Report by the Sound of Silence Group (SoS). Retrieved from: https://15julyfacts.com/sadat/(Accession: 25 May 2018).

de Soysa, I. (2017). Predatory Government and the Feasibility of Rebellion: A Micro Logic of the Capitalist Peace. Printed from the *Oxford Research*

Encyclopedia of Politics. USA: Oxford University Press.

Spencer, L. (2018). The ECtHR and Post-coup Turkey: Losing Ground or Losing Credibility? *VerfBlog*, 2018/7/17. doi: https: //doi. org/10.17 176/20 1 80 717 – 102 034 – 23. (Accession: 7 August 2018).

Sufrin, C. (2017). *Jailcare: Finding the Safety Net for Women Behind Bars*. Oakland, CA: University of California Press.

Tilly, C. & Tarrow, S. (2015). *Contentious Politics (Second revised edition)*. New York: Oxford University Press.

Tilly, C. (1998). *Durable Inequality*. Berkeley, Los Angeles, CA: University of California Press.

Tilly, C. (2003). *The Politics of Collective Violence*. Cambridge, UK: Cambridge University Press.

Tilly, C. (2007). *Democracy*. New York, NY: Cambridge University Press.

Transparency International (2009). *The Anti-Corruption Plain Language Guide. Retrieved from:* http: //www. transparency. org/whatwedo/pub/the_ant_corrupton_plain_language_guide (Accession: 20 October 2018).

Turbeville, B. (2015). US/*Turkey Sign Deal to Arm Death Squads in Syria*. Retrieved from: http: //www. brandonturbeville. com/2015/02/usturkey-sign-deal-to-arm-death-squads. html (Accession: 23 May 2018).

TutsakBebekler [@TutsakBebekler]. (14 11. 2018). Ayşe Şeyma Taş 2 gün önce 25 günlük bebeğiyle tutuklanıp Ferizli cezaevine konuldu. "Yapmayın" dedikleri hakim "bebeği niye doğurdun" diye azarlamış! ! ! [Tweet]. Retrieved from: https: //mobile. twitter. com/TutsakBebekler/status/10626285931 140 940 802

UNICEF (2012). *Integrated Social Protection Systems: Enhancing Equity for Children* (Social Protection Strategic Framework). New York, NY: United Nations Children's Fund.

Ur, J. (2014). Households and the Emergence of Cities in Ancient Mesopotamia. *Cambridge Archaeological Journal, 24* (02), 249 – 268. doi: 10.1017/ s095977431400047x.

Vahabi, M. (2016). *A Positive Theory of Predatory State*. Paper accepted for presentation in 2016 Conference of the Society for Institutional & Organizational Economics (SIOE), Sciences Po, Paris, France, on June 15 – 17, 2016.

Venice Commission (2016). *Turkey: Opinion on Emergency Decree Laws Nos. 667 – 676 Adopted Following the Failed Coup of 15 July 2016*. Opinion No. 865/2016 by the Venice Commission of the CoE. Retrieved from: http: //www. venice. coe. int/webforms/documents/default. aspx? pdffile=C-DL-AD(2016)037-e (Accession: 7 August 2018).

Weiss, L. (1998). *The Myth of the Powerless State: Governing the Economy in a Global Era*. New York, NY: Polity Press.

WVS (2015). *World Values Survey (2010–2014): Crossings by Country*. Retrieved from: http: //www. worldvaluessurvey. org/WVSDocumentationWV6. jsp (Accession: 5 February 2018).

Yellinek, R. (2018). Erdoğan's Private Militia. *Platform for Peace and Justice (PPJ)*. Retrieved from: http: //www. platformpj. org/Erdoğans-private-militia/(Accession: 23 May 2018).

Yılmaz, K. (2017). Was Gülen Really 'Once a Close Ally' of Erdoğan? *Platform for Peace and Justice (PPJ)*. Retrieved from: http: //www. platformpj. org/Gülen-really-close-ally-Erdoğan/(Accession: **31 October 2018**).

INDEX

A

Access to Information 33
Adverse Opinion 94
AKP xxxix, 15, 44, 47, 48, 57, 58, 67, 93, 96, 97, 98, 99, 100, 102, 103, 131, 139, 144, 152, 172, 175, 185, 186, 187, 195, 197
Al-Badr 152
Al-Nusra 135
al-Qaida 150
Amnesty International 22
Anatolian Agency 164
Ancient Mesopotamia 192, 210
Ansor 152
anthropology
   anthropological 18, 28
asset value xxxix
authoritarian
   authoritarianism xliii, 97, 99, 159, 173, 188, 189, 194, 195, 196, 197, 199, 200, 206, 207
autocratic
   autocrat xliii, 48, 88, 99, 193

B

Bank Asya 13, 55, 56, 171
black laws 155, 157, 159
blacklisting
   blacklisted 36, 37, 38, 39, 40
burden of proof 8, 53, 155
Bureaucra-cide 112
bureaucratic oligarchy 188
burial services xxxviii
ByLock 13
bystander reaction 18, 19

C

Cabinet Decree 4, 52, 68, 69, 72, 75, 93, 95
Capital Tax 46, 204
cataloguing 37, 38, 39, 179, 181
Chief Executive President 166
children xxxvii, xlii, 14, 15, 16, 18, 19, 20, 21, 23, 27, 31, 107, 171
Child-Sensitive Social Protection 20
citizenship 21, 29, 35, 138
civic exclusion 36
civil death xxxviii, 6, 28, 29, 30, 32, 35, 36, 37, 40
civil war 5, 131
cliental network 189
clientelism 100, 199
co-habitation 175
comfort zone 160, 191, 192
concentration of power 8, 190, 191, 193
Constitution
   Turkish Constitution 17, 80, 109, 111, 114, 167, 173, 174, 176, 185
Constitutional Court
   AYM x, 37, 48, 109, 111, 114, 119, 120, 121, 122, 168, 185
corruption xl, 44, 63, 64, 72, 84, 90, 92, 97, 101, 102, 106, 107, 172, 183, 198, 204
Corruption Perception Index 101
Council of Europe
   CoE xlii, 116, 123, 125, 126,

210
Council of Judges and Prosecutors
  HSK 48, 111, 114, 170, 183, 184, 185
Council of Ministers 176, 177
Council of State 114, 183, 184, 185
Court of Cassation 183, 184, 185
cultural ecology 97, 102, 104
culture of impunity 156, 160
cuneiform 27, 192

D

death squads xlii, xliii, 101, 131, 133, 135, 139, 140, 141, 142, 143, 148, 154, 159
Decree Law 33, 39, 40, 50, 51, 54, 56, 57, 69, 92, 93, 111, 113, 116, 117, 120, 136, 155, 157, 168, 177, 178, 180, 181, 184, 185
defence industry 147, 149
Defence Industry Support Fund 69
Dehumanization 18
Dei Gratia
  a gift from God 19, 109
deniability 39, 135, 140, 143
detention 3, 8, 13, 14, 19, 131, 155
Direct Forfeiture 50
disenfranchisement 36, 139, 208
dismissal 3, 5, 8, 30, 31, 32, 33, 39, 113, 117, 118, 123, 176, 183
dispossession 3, 8
DUP
  Directly Unproductive Profit-seeking 49, 59, 191, 204

E

economic survival 196
Economic Value of Peace 133
economy of power 160
Electoral Authoritarianism 99, 208, 209
Electoral Autocracy 194, 199
  EA 194
electoral democracy 44, 194
Ergenekon 102
Euphrates Shield 133
EU Progress Report 112, 206
European Convention on Human Rights
  ECHR 17, 111, 119, 125, 126, 154, 207
European Court of Human Rights
  ECtHR xli, xlii, 114, 116, 118, 119, 120, 121, 122, 123, 124, 125, 126, 205, 206, 207, 210
Executive Presidency xliii, 166
expungement 36

F

family business 75, 182, 193
Fethullahist Terror Organisation
  FETO 13, 52, 56, 110
forfeiture xxxix, xl, 8, 44, 45, 46, 47, 48, 49, 51, 52, 53, 54, 57, 58, 59, 191
Friday sermons 96, 168

G

gastro-politic 27, 28, 48, 200
General Chairman 185
genocide 30, 31
Gezi Park 105, 151
Global Financial Integrity 140
good governance 187, 189, 200
Governors 171, 177
grand corruption xl, 55, 75, 97
Grand National Assembly
    TBMM 48, 168, 169, 172, 174, 175, 184, 186
guilt by association 16, 37, 170
Gülenist 3, 4, 6, 7, 10, 15, 34, 35, 97, 104, 105, 110, 130, 131, 156
Gülen Movement 3, 4, 5, 9, 10, 13, 14, 16, 19, 39, 49, 50, 51, 52, 53, 54, 55, 56, 57, 94, 104, 110, 111, 170, 171

H

hatred 22, 103, 151, 156, 160
homicide 29, 131
Homo sacer 29, 131, 204
hot money 8, 140
Human Rights Watch 22
hunger strike 25, 26
Hunger Strike 25

I

imam-hatip 97
immunity 52, 65, 94, 131, 151, 153, 154, 156, 157, 159, 161
impunity effect 131, 159
Indirect Forfeiture by Trustee 52
inequality 197
Inquiry Commission 40, 113, 116

International Forum of Sovereign Wealth Funds
    IFSWF 66
Interpellation (Gensoru) 173
intimidation
    intimidate xlii, 165
ISIL 133, 135, 137, 150
Islam xli, 46, 96, 97, 99, 129, 145
    Islamic 15, 16, 33, 93, 96, 97, 101, 137, 148, 149
Islamist xlii, 3, 6, 7, 47, 58, 96, 99, 102, 103, 104, 129, 130, 134, 145, 149, 151, 152

J

jail xxxviii, 7, 13, 22
Jamaat-el-Islami 152
jihadist
    jihadist groups xlii, 133, 135, 136, 137, 138, 148, 150, 182
JİTEM 129, 136

K

killable bodies xxxviii
Köksal v. Turkey 120, 122, 123, 124, 125, 126
Koza İpek 54, 57
Kurdish 35, 133, 137, 139, 151, 154, 156, 165
Kurds 102, 105, 141

L

legitimacy 129, 135, 196
Linaburg-Maduell Transparency Index
    LMTI 64
longue durée 189, 190
Losers' Consent 163, 204

M

macho cultures 151
March for Justice 17
Media and Law Studies Association 125
media outlets xl, 6, 50, 53, 112, 117, 151, 168, 187
middle-income trap 100
murder 155
Muslim
 Muslims xxxviii, 15, 21, 45, 46, 47, 96, 97, 146, 152, 159

N

Nahdat-ul-Ulama 152
National Estates xxxix, 50, 69
National Intelligence
 MİT 35, 37, 39, 136, 143, 145, 152, 179, 181, 182
National Outlook
 Milli Görüş 47
National Security Council
 MGK 30, 115, 171, 181
neo-Ottomanist 132
nominally democratic institutions 195

O

Official Gazette x, 4, 18, 33, 40, 46, 52, 53, 58, 65, 68, 69, 72, 74, 75, 80, 110, 111, 114, 115, 136, 154, 164, 168, 169, 170, 176, 177, 178, 179, 180, 181, 183, 184
Olive Branch 133, 138, 145
opposition xlii, xliii, 14, 48, 88, 103, 105, 137, 138, 139, 143, 145, 150, 151, 160, 168, 186, 188, 197, 198, 199, 200, 201

Organised Legislative Operations xxxvii, 160
Ottoman Hearths 150, 151

P

Palace xliii, 7, 74, 75, 76, 89, 107, 161, 167, 173, 174, 175, 176, 177, 179, 180, 181, 182, 185, 186, 187, 189, 193, 195, 197, 198, 199, 200, 202
Palatial Boards 179
Palatial Offices 179
Palatial regime xliii, 7, 36, 58, 173, 175, 177, 180, 190, 191, 193, 195, 201
Panopticon 179
paramilitary xli, xlii, xliii, 101, 132, 136, 137, 140, 141, 143, 145, 147, 150, 151, 152, 153, 159, 205
parliament
 parliamentary xliv, 65, 70, 80, 110, 114, 138, 155, 167, 175, 176, 177, 187, 195, 206
party-member president 185, 186
patrimonial property 167
Penal Judges of Peace 53
Pentagon 137
piety 7, 98, 186, 195
pious xxxviii, 15, 25, 96, 97, 98
PKK 102, 137, 141
Platform for Peace and Justice
 PPJ xi, 211
plundering 88, 106, 159
polarization 102, 104, 105
poverty xli, 28, 99, 100, 101, 102, 202
predatory xl, xli, 7, 65, 71, 84, 88, 89, 90, 91, 95, 96, 99, 102,

104, 107, 179, 191
pregnant women
mothers xxxvii, xxxviii, xlii, 18, 22
Presidential Circular 180, 181
Presidential Decision 75, 145, 179, 182
Presidential Decree 57, 74, 100, 176, 178, 181, 182
presidential veto 175
prison
prisons 18, 35, 36, 165
provisional village guards
security guards xliii, 135, 156

Q

Quick expropriation 52

R

Reichstag Fire 167
reinstate xli, 113
Religious Affairs
Diyanet 33, 96, 97
religious groups 103
rule of law 4, 140, 160

S

SADAT xliii, 131, 141, 142, 143, 144, 145, 146, 147, 148, 149, 150, 151, 152, 159, 209
safety net 17, 34, 202
Santiago Principles xl, 64, 72, 84
Savings Deposit Insurance Fund
TMSF xxxix, 50, 54, 55, 56, 57, 58, 171, 181
Shepherd-flock game 8, 161

social movements xli, 9, 102, 104, 202
Solidarity Foundation for the Martyr Relatives and Veterans 93
sovereign power 30
Sovereign Wealth Fund
SWF 62, 63, 64, 66, 71, 72, 73, 75, 76, 78, 80, 81, 83, 84
state fetishism 97, 98
State of Emergency
SoE xxxvii, xxxviii, xli, xlii, 4, 6, 15, 17, 25, 30, 36, 38, 40, 49, 54, 55, 58, 92, 95, 97, 105, 106, 109, 112, 113, 114, 116, 157, 165, 167, 168, 169, 170, 171, 172, 177, 199
stigmatisation
stigmatised xxxviii
subordination xliv, 8, 159, 167
suffering xli, 22, 28
Supreme Board of Election xi, 164
suspension 112, 113, 170
sympathy xxxviii, xlii, 10, 160
Syria xlii, 91, 105, 131, 133, 136, 137, 141, 145, 160, 182, 210

T

tarikats 6
terrorist organisations 170
theft 83, 98, 140
The Guy has won 163
Train-and-Equip program xlii, 132, 137, 138, 182
Transparency International xl, 75, 101, 156, 172, 208, 210
trustee (kayyım) xxxviii, 5, 49, 52, 53, 54, 56, 92, 171
Turkey Wealth Fund

TWF xxxix, xl, 65, 66, 67, 68, 69, 70, 71, 72, 73, 74, 75, 76, 77, 78, 79, 81, 82, 83, 84, 93, 94, 95, 182
Turkification 45
Turkish Code of Civil Servants 113
Turkish Code of Penal Procedure
TCPP xxxix, 53
Turkish Court of Accounts
TCA 70, 79, 80
Turkish Education Foundation (Türkiye Maarif Vakfı) xi, 52, 94, 95

U

Ultranationalist 3, 6
unaccountability 157
undemocratic 194, 201
United States 47, 61, 176, 193, 195
Unmanned Combat Aerial Vehicles 182
usual suspects 172

V

Vakıfbank 93
variegated citizenship 35
Venice Commission xli, xlii, 116, 121, 210
victimisation 130
victims xxxviii, xli, xlii, 3, 7, 8, 15, 19, 21, 25, 40, 109, 110, 114, 116, 118, 123, 125, 126, 134, 160
vigilant
vigilant groups xlii, xliii
vigilante

vigilante groups 142, 143, 157
violence xxxviii, xli, xlii, 6, 7, 15, 88, 89, 99, 105, 130, 133, 134, 135, 138, 139, 140, 141, 154, 155, 159, 160, 192, 202
vulnerability 15, 32, 202

W

war on terror 95, 105, 154, 168, 188

Z

Zihni v. Turkey 119, 120, 121

FIGURES

Figure 1: Alleged coup plotters are being taken to trial in a ritualised order
Source: (AFP, 2017)

Figure 2: To be a "social movement": Gülen sympathizers as protesters shouting slogans outside the headquarters of Bugün newspaper and Kanaltürk TV station in Istanbul, in a demonstration for press freedom **Source:** (Ozan Kose/AFP via Getty Images, 2016)

Figure 3: Fadime G. detained right after she delivered birth in Alanya
Source: (Haberler.com, 2017)

Figure 4: Babies in the Ereğli Prison, Konya
Source: (BBC Turkish, 2017)

Figure 5: Nuriye G. and Semih Ö. In hunger strike
Source: (Altan Gocker/Barcroft Images, 2017)

Figure 6: Koza İpek Company surrounded by the Police to enforce the court's order of forfeiture
Source: (Hürriyet, 2016)

Figures | 223

Figure 7: State-owned companies within the portfolio of the TWF
Source: (TWF, 2017)

Figure 8: Food distribution by the Metropolitan Municipality of Ankara
Source: (ankara.bel.tr, 2016)

Figure 9: HQ of the European Court of Human Rights, Strasbourg
Source: (coe.int, 2018)

Figure 10: "If she is martyred, we do shroud her body with flag," Erdoğan says in Kahramanmaraş meeting
Source: (Avrupa Forum, 2018).

Figure 11: Pro-Erdoğan jihadist groups in Syria
Source: (DHA-Depo photos, 2018)

Figure 12: Artist and journalist Zehra Doğan, modelling on of a real photo taken after the military operations, painted Nusaybin in ruin with Turkish flags flying above
Source: (Hyperallergic, 2018).

Figure 13: Soldiers who were not aware they were part of the coup are beaten by unidentified civilians on the FSM Bridge, Istanbul
Source: (Reuters, 2016)

Figure 14: Cartoonist C. Latuff depicted the 24 June elections in Turkey
Source: (latuffcartoons.wordpress.com, 2018)

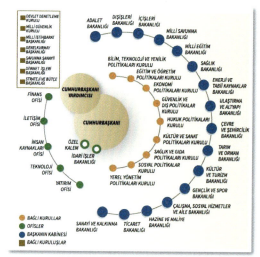

Figure 16: Palatial Regime from the Eyes of its Supporters
Source: Cumhuriyet (20 June 2018)

Figure 18: Erdoğan and two of the opposition leaders, K. Kılıçdaroğlu of CHP (left) and M. Akşener of IYI Party (right), at the Mausoleum of Atatürk
Source: (Takvim, 2018)